BEST CANADIAN ESSAYS 2025

Edited by Emily Urquhart

Biblioasis
Windsor, Ontario

FIRST EDITION
ISBN 978-1-77196-636-8 (Trade Paper)
ISBN 978-1-77196-637-5 (eBook)

Guest edited by Emily Urquhart
Copyedited by Martin Ainsley
Series designed by Ingrid Paulson

Published with the generous assistance of the Canada Council for the Arts, which last year invested $153 million to bring the arts to Canadians throughout the country, and the financial support of the Government of Canada. Biblioasis also acknowledges the support of the Ontario Arts Council (OAC), an agency of the Government of Ontario, which last year funded 1,709 individual artists and 1,078 organizations in 204 communities across Ontario, for a total of $52.1 million, and the contribution of the Government of Ontario through the Ontario Book Publishing Tax Credit and Ontario Creates.

PRINTED AND BOUND IN CANADA

CONTENTS

Emily Urquhart

~~~~~~~~~

INTRODUCTION

A few years ago, I memorized the final section of Robert Penn Warren's long poem, *Audubon: A Vision*, and ever since, the first lines will occasionally drum through my mind the way a song lyric might: *Tell me a story / In this century, and moment, of mania / Tell me a story*. Over the four seasons that I read and compiled the essays in this collection, these verses often surfaced, playing on an internal loop. We are in a century and moment of mania and what better way to explore and illuminate this state than an essay?

In tackling the role of editor for the *Best Canadian Essays* series I read work in literary and journalism magazines, in newspapers, online journals and zines, and in publications that I couldn't begin to classify. How many essays? Maybe hundreds. I am not a spreadsheet person. I tracked my progress through sticky notes and marginalia, and by the precarious piles of magazines stacked on my office floor, which shot up like skyscrapers in a fast-developing city. This vast reading was an act of divination, and software would only have interfered. Weaving around the magazine towers and returning to their sticky-noted and marked-up pages, I sought to understand what a reader wants from an essay. Content, regardless of how our algorithmic-addled brains may feel these days, is not key. A skilled writer can illuminate any corner of our universe. It was how they did so that interested me. What made one work on parenthood, or grief, or immigration rise above another was in the writer's delivery. It was the keen observations, the choices made on what to bring forth and what to leave behind, the surprising turn, inventive language, and the power to stir emotion. I wasn't looking to define the genre—many have tried and failed valiantly—I was asking, to paraphrase Sheila Heti, How should an essay be?

I kept a running tally of ways, written longform in my notebook, which included some of the following: An essay can be a narrative, lament, letter, or poem. An essay might rant, hold strong opinions, or be a call to action. It can be futile, or constructive, or both. It can be personal and distant all at once. It can entertain, instruct, or educate. It can resonate. It can resolve, or it can fade into the ether. It can laugh. It can weep. It can howl with indignity. Essays, I concluded, are changeable and chameleon-like; they adapt with the times, and they reinvent themselves.

After nearly a year of reading, a cluster of singular works came forth. These essays were disparate in their content, joined only by their shared publishing year, 2023, and the strength of their execution. I emerged in early spring with a list of fifteen works from twelve publications. Then, I began to play with their order of appearance. Loose categories would form and just as quickly dissolve. I might group works under "childhood" but realize that they could equally be classified as essays about love, family, or identity. Ultimately, I organized the works by how they interacted. Some flocked together, and others acted as a call and response or echoed one another's themes. Many danced; none touched. This collection begins and ends with two authors whose work has long been a testament to the best writing in our country, and this happened naturally and at the same time felt appropriate, necessary. Helen Humphreys leads us in, and Katherine Ashenburg guides us out. All I did was gather, as if arranging a bouquet of wildflowers or hanging a selection of artworks on a wall; however, I feel immensely proud of this collection.

From the first line of "The Boiler Room," by Helen Humphreys, the reader is compelled to know more. Humphreys reveals her most embarrassing moment, and it is humorous—at first. Then, she parses and expands the moment, and as with the best essays, the piece ends in revelation for both reader and writer.

This is followed by Jiin Kim's "Complimentary, Free of Charge," in which the "gravy-coloured interior" of a chain restaurant is the site of a cultural inauguration for an immigrant family from Korea. It is a child's story, remembered and told from a distance, yet the scenes feel fresh and immediate.

In "We Are All Animals at Night," Lana Hall writes a haunting piece on the five years she spent working nights at a massage parlour. The story is less about the work, and more a focus on the community that forms amongst her colleagues and other night-shift workers in what she calls an "ecosystem" of mutual care. What the body betrays and what the body withstands is also explored with wit and a poet's precision in "Rotten," Ariel Gordon's essay on dendrological and gynecological disease. "I sit on the stairs with my rotten cervix, my sexually transmitted angst, and watch the tree move and not move. We not-move together."

In "Birth Stories, Adoption, and Myths," Vance Wright calls their birth story "a mythic speech act," a description that might equally apply to the polyphonic approach they take in this moving essay on transracial adoption. Wright seeks a single origin story but finds many, in part because "adoption is a process, an experience, a practice, that resists neat narratives, genres, and stable categorizations."

Identity is also the focus of "My Struggle and 'My Struggle,'" by James Cairns in which a devoted reading of Karl Ove Knausgaard's series of autobiographical novels reveals how reading is an act of engagement that can also reflect the reader's emotional and lived state. Cairns was speaking of the books he chose to read, but I felt it applied equally to *how* a person reads. For example, in my role as editor for this series, I read differently than I would for pleasure or research. I was not simply a reader, I was an explorer, a pile maker, a list maker, a decision maker, sometimes feeling certain, other times wavering. What I learned was that I needed to approach every reading session in a generous emotional state. It was my best shot at being fair. I am a writer of essays, too, and I know what reins must be harnessed to get these strange beasts into form. From the first thrilling spark to the endurance needed to revise, and revise again, to the act of publication when your carefully crafted thoughts are available to anyone who might chance upon them, including your judgmental aunt and your first-grade teacher. That takes a toll on a person, and with every entry into a new essay I acknowledged this weight.

At one point, I feared I had included too many "authors" in my growing list of essays for this collection. This ridiculous concern occurred deep into the process. I was suffering a kind of editorial break. I'd briefly lost the plot. Would I have feared there were too many poets in a poetry anthology, or fiction writers in a short-story anthology? No, I would not. For this reason, the writing life is woven through a number of these pieces, sometimes in the background, but other times as the main feature, as in Tom Rachman's hilarious essay, "Confessions of a Literary Schlub," about the grim and often absurd act of book promotion. As Rachman arrives at his empty reading event in the Cayman Islands, the bookseller suggests that he swim with the stingrays the following day, because "they always turn up." As a writer, I related to Rachman's essay, but you don't need to be a literary schlub to delight in its humour.

The next essay, "Found," by Sadiqa de Meijer, is about the exquisite pain of a writer losing her notebook. (Horrifying! I would rather lose my cellphone or wallet!) Months later, fragmented phrases come to de Meijer from the lost notebook, but they remain just outside her grasp. In this disappearance, she has lost the "gleanings" of her life, including "serial attempts at describing the sounds of pigeons cooing. Names of movies to see and books to read. How I felt in the hour before reuniting with a favourite teacher after almost two decades. The woman walking with a large, ornate wooden crucifix on her shoulder who paused and winked at me."

The literary theme continues with "The 'Beauty' of My Existence," by Rebecca Kempe. It is the story of an artistic act—in this case a poem read aloud at a high-school literary-arts coffee house—that siphons the author into a role she cannot escape, as she is forced to perform the piece over and over at subsequent events. The enforced repetition has the ring of an ancient myth, but this story is of our time. "This is the problem with being Black and being an artist: whenever you exist in mainstream places, it can never just be about your art," writes Kempe.

Besides writing, a second theme that cropped up in my reading was parenthood and childhood, and the best works left me changed, imprinted with images and new thoughts on a subject as old as time. In "Shadow Face," Jessica Moore explores the permeability of motherhood—from what might enter the body through the opening of a surgical knife to the dissolution of a mother's previous lives and identities after the birth of a child.

Michelle Cyca's piece, "Big Babies," focuses on children in public spaces. She asks the reader whether we consider children members of society with the right to exist as they are. Children are friction in the environment, Cyca writes, but "it's only temporary good fortune that prevents any of us from becoming the friction in someone else's existence."

The final four essays in this collection address various forms of loss. In "Now Must Say Goodbye," by Christine Lai, the author collects and contemplates postcards "in a time of dispersal." In one scene she finds that superimposing these miniature images on a living landscape can change her memory of what happened in that space. I had never considered the postcard as agency before. It is a surprising, elegiac piece.

The following essay, "The Breathing Lands," by Leanne Betasamosake Simpson, is a sorrowful and poetic rendering of a complicated reunion. "What you are asking of me, you cannot give in return," the author writes in this intimate address to a "you" that is never revealed. What becomes clear, however, is that the lives of author and subject are intertwined, and that the distance between them is both an act of protection and one of love.

I have read Mitchell Consky's "Notes from Grief Camp" several times, and I never get through a scene about a camp icebreaker without weeping. Young campers are corralled into groups by superficial choices such as liking chocolate ice cream and swimming, but the categories gradually grow more serious until they are grouped by the death of a specific loved one—a sibling or a parent. There is devastation in each individual loss and yet in this gathering, at a summer camp for grieving children, there is a sense of belonging. This is also true for the author, who lost his father as a young adult and writes eloquently about the complexities of grief.

Mourning, rather than grief, is the topic of the final essay, "How We Said Goodbye," by Katherine Ashenburg, a stirring meditation on the importance of gathering after loss. The story focuses on the death of her friend and fellow writer, Anne Kingston, at the onset of the pandemic. The plans for a memorial were halted by public-health restrictions, the celebration waylaid for years. Mourning was put on pause. When Ashenburg writes, "Standing in the presence of other mourners, even in a crowd of mostly strangers, is oddly crucial," I imagine the little boys from the previous essay nodding in agreement.

*

I carried the magazines that housed these fifteen essays in a woven straw basket with two sturdy handles. Mostly, I carted them from where I work at the kitchen table to my office in the attic. Occasionally, we travelled farther. They weighed enough to set off my station wagon's seatbelt alarm. What I'm saying is that when I had to haul the essays with me to children's sporting events or weekends away, my car thought they were human. This is fitting, because together these essays are a portrait of humanity, one that accompanied me through many months. The characters, ideas, arguments, and thoughts floated to the top of my mind's pool, not just when I was reading, but when I was doing other things—walking the dog in the forest, riding the train to work, folding laundry, or taking one of those long drives—and this is how I knew these essayists belonged here. I asked for something—*Tell me a story/In this century, and moment, of mania/Tell me a story*—and they answered my call.

Helen Humphreys

THE BOILER ROOM

One of the more embarrassing moments of my life took place at my high school reunion. A group of us were reminiscing about the alternative school where we had once been students. *Remember when Derek jumped off the roof? Remember the principal's dog? Remember the small doors on the bathroom stalls because the building had once been a primary school?*

"Remember," I said, "how we would go to the boiler room and neck with the janitor?"

There was silence where a moment ago there had been laughter and overlapping voices.

Ah, right, I thought. *So that only happened to me.*

The janitor, E., was old. He had a long, grey beard and always wore an engineer's cap to cover his bald head. He rode a motorcycle and grew exotic plants in the glass corridor that served as the school student lounge. He tended many flowers there, but he was most proud of his bird of paradise, with its extravagant orange bloom that resembled the crest on a crane's head.

The boiler room was separate from the school. You had to cross the parking lot behind the building to get to it. The room was windowless and dark, and half of it was taken up with the enormous boiler that clanked and hissed like a cranky beast.

E. had a desk in the boiler room, and a chair beside it, where I would sometimes sit. I have a photograph of myself in that chair, aged seventeen, taken by E. on one of those occasions. On the cinderblock wall above the chair was a poster with a photograph of a train and the words, *Life is a journey, not a destination.*

I don't remember when I first went to the boiler room, or why. I must have been invited there by E., but I don't remember. I do, however, remember the kisses. They were long and deep and I can still bring back the feel of his soft beard on my open mouth and the sprung camber of his ribs against my chest. We kissed for a long time on each visit, pressed close together, and only broke apart when there was a noise in the hallway that signaled someone's approach.

I didn't initiate the kisses, or invite them, but I didn't stop them either. Because they never progressed to groping or sex, because they weren't coupled with any of the sweaty urgency I was used to in boys my own age, I wasn't afraid of them. I knew that they weren't innocent, but I thought that they were harmless.

At seventeen, I knew I wanted to be a writer. I was already working on this with intent and tilting my whole future in that direction. I knew, from reading, that good writing came out of experience, and so I was eager to have experiences and rarely refused anything that promised to be one. I suppose this is why I allowed those kisses to happen in the first place and why, even though I don't think I ever enjoyed them, I felt reconciled to them. But here is the question I ask myself now—what is the line between adventure and trespass? While I knew, more or less, what I was doing with E. in the boiler room, what did he think he was doing with me?

We saw one another outside of school hours. He came to my house and met my mother. I remember him smoking his roll-up cigarettes at our picnic bench in the backyard and that he stayed for dinner. When my mother went into the house to fetch something, he said, *You never need go to seed like your mother.* My mother wasn't even forty and looked great.

He often drove me past a certain fish-and-chips shop in his car. His middle son had killed himself in the apartment above the shop. It pained him to remember the death, but he couldn't stop himself from driving by and looking up to the second-floor window. He rubbed his face with one of his gnarly workman's hands to soothe himself. He had been the one to find his son's body.

I had just bought my first motorcycle on installment and so we would ride our bikes together around the countryside near where we both lived. Once we went out to visit E.'s brother who lived as a hermit on land that didn't belong to him. His cabin was uphill and across some fields. The track uphill was rutted and would have been impassable in a car. The bikes barely managed it.

The hermit brother was surly and taciturn, bad at having company. E. tried to cajole him into being more sociable while I was there, but he only grudgingly made us a cup of tea. His cabin was low-ceilinged and dark. It had snowshoes and skis lashed to the ceiling and a fireplace made of fieldstones loosely mortared together. E. had brought his brother some tinned food on our visit. *He has shellshock,* he said, when we were leaving. *From the war.*

E. had also been in World War II, although it hadn't had the same effect on him. He was born in 1918, which made him forty-three years older than me.

E. knew another hermit, who lived in the woods near a race-track and survived on the leftover bits of hotdogs and buns that he scavenged from garbage cans on race days. He toasted them over his fire to make them more palatable. Eventually he got colon cancer and died, probably from years of eating only hotdogs and white buns. E. used to call his friend *the other grey beard.*

*

Once, we rode our bikes out to visit his younger son, who lived with his wife and children about a half hour north of the hermit brother. The son and his wife had a grey parrot that flapped around a huge cage in the kitchen, and two dogs that freely roamed the property. The son was upset with his father for bringing me there and they had a fight about it in the kitchen. I went outside and raced the dogs through the cornfields.

When I think about that day now, it seems obvious that the father and son were fighting because this had happened before; E. had turned up with some other very young woman to visit his son. If it had never happened before, the son would have appeared shocked, but not so immediately outraged. His anger suggested a pattern.

And I had always believed, right up until that moment at my high school reunion, that I wasn't the only one who was kissing E. I had assumed that other female students were also visiting with him in the boiler room, and somehow that normalized it and just made it seem part of the alternative school experience.

Now, of course, I can't believe how gullible I was, and I can see how E. had most of the power. But there were also many moments when he wasn't kissing me, and in those moments, we were talking, or he was showing me his garden, or we were riding our bikes together, and in those moments I enjoyed his friendship.

When E. retired from the school, I used to go and visit him at his house. He was long divorced and I'm not sure what had become of his wife. He never talked about her. But he had the family home, a one and a half storey brick house in the neighbourhood next to the one where I lived with my parents. There was a double lot at the back of the house where he grew vegetables. The front door was far from the street and was shadowed by two pine trees.

I went there once a week, ostensibly to eat my lunch with E, but we began kissing pretty much the moment I got there. At his house, since he lived alone, we were rarely interrupted, and the kissing sessions lasted well over an hour. The kissing was more focused, and I could sense a shift in it. It was becoming more intense. He liked to press our bodies together and have us breathe in unison. I wondered then if we might end up sleeping together.

But, as it turned out, I only went to see E. at his house a few times. School was over for me and I had started working at a full-service car wash downtown. I worked eleven-and-a-half-hour shifts and had no free time during the day anymore. When I wasn't at work I was sleeping, because the job was exhausting.

E. died of cancer not too many years afterwards. I don't think he made seventy. My mother told me the news over the phone. She had seen his obituary in the local paper and thought I would want to know because we had once been friends. It surprised me because, even though I knew he was old, he had always seemed so full of vitality and far from death.

It is hard, with the vagaries of memory, and the shift in societal attitudes between then and now, to know what to think about that episode in my life. For all my writerly hankering after experience, it is an experience I have never written about, until now, and I have only written about it because I have started to think about that line between adventure and trespass.

So, which is it?

When I am writing a novel, I sometimes try and think of the one true thing that is at the heart of the story, a thing that will remain true no matter how I turn it, no matter how much I look at it. So, when I turn this story of myself and E., what is the one true thing in it?

I think it is that moment when E. and I were visiting his youngest son and they started fighting. I knew at the time it was about me, but I didn't want to participate in the exchange. I couldn't be bothered. It felt like any of the times adults would argue in front of me. I didn't want to stand there and listen to them. I went outside to play with the dogs.

And that's how I know I was a child.

And that's how I know it was trespass.

Jiin Kim

COMPLIMENTARY, FREE OF CHARGE

Ueta-san had the excellent posture and the slightly raised shoulders of many short men. He took off his aviator sunglasses and sized up the restaurant. In the parking lot, we stood behind him, facing a replica of a two-storey Alpine lodge, complete with flower boxes in bloom. In his fashionable platform running shoes, cloaked by his long bell-bottomed jeans, he advanced toward the charming building like he wanted to conquer it. His lovely wife and my family followed him like loyal foot soldiers through the doors of Swiss Chalet.

Even though my family had been in Canada for a couple of years, we had never eaten in a sit-down restaurant with waitresses. With both of my parents working near-minimum-wage factory jobs, there was no surplus for extravagances such as dining out. And just as importantly, we lacked the confidence to order from an unfamiliar menu. If Ueta-san hadn't called and invited us today, we wouldn't have had the courage to come to a restaurant.

The downstairs dining area was near capacity. Once we were seated in the non-smoking section, our eyes roved around the room, which had none of the visual allure of the exterior of the building. I could only surmise that the Swiss loved the colour brown. There was dark wood panelling on the walls and brown tiles on the floor. Even the mouth-watering aroma of flame-cooked meat, stirred with the scent of tobacco from the smoking section, evoked the dark warm tone. My two younger, school-aged sisters, sitting across from me, pressed their slight bodies toward each other, looking small in the cavernous room.

Our waitress looked to be in her early forties. Or she might have been an exhausted woman in her thirties. Her hair was in a ponytail, and she had a layered and feathered mane around her face, otherwise known as the trendy Farrah Fawcett haircut. Farrah was an actress on the popular TV show *Charlie's Angels*, where three gorgeous private detectives in high heels chased down criminals who ran even slower than they did. Our Chalet Farrah wore sensible shoes.

"What can I get you folks to drink?"

My mom asked no one in particular, "Free?"

Ueta-san rephrased the question to the waitress, "Included with food?"

"No, it's separate." Chalet Farrah folded Ueta-san's menu and pointed with her pen to the drink prices on the back.

My sisters and I stared at our mom for the go-ahead. We knew better than to order anything without her approval, otherwise there would be a verbal blitzkrieg at home followed by the cold-shoulder campaign.

After the waitress left with our drink orders, we studied the menu like we'd be tested on it. "Huh, they *only* have chicken,"

Ueta-san said. I found his comment odd since I had assumed he had been to Swiss Chalet before.

My parents, who bellowed like co-dictators at home, spoke with diffidence, "What will you have, Ueta-san?" After a discussion among the adults, it was decided that the two men, Ueta-san and my dad, would get the half chicken with fries, and the women and children would get the quarter chicken with fries.

The waitress returned and placed our fizzy drinks on the table. "Ready to order?"

We waited for Ueta-san to speak first. "Half chicken with fries," he said in a thick Japanese accent. One by one, we placed our order.

Ueta-san was younger than my parents, but they looked up to him because he had been in Canada for many years, and he was a supervisor at the factory where my dad worked. He was Japanese, and his wife was Korean like us. Childless, they doted upon my sisters and me. The couple had met in their youth, when they both had lived in Argentina with their respective families. Not knowing each other's native language, they spoke to each other in Spanish. While his wife made efforts to learn Japanese, Ueta-san said he would not learn Korean, because he preferred the dulcet sound of his native language to the strident tone of Korean.

Japanese may be easier on the ear, but it was harshly forced upon Koreans during the decades of occupation, before 1945. Since Japanese was the only language allowed to be taught in school during those years, my parents spoke it fluently. My sisters and I spoke English to Ueta-san. When we were all together, up to four languages were spoken at once, but somehow we understood each other.

The waitress came back with seven meals and placed a white, steam-trailing bowl of reddish-brown liquid speckled with spices beside each of them. "Enjoy," she said before leaving.

We all stared at the mystery bowls. "What's this?" I asked.

After a second of consideration, Ueta-san said, "Soup."

My mom said worriedly, "We didn't order soup."

"It's complimentary, that's why the bowls are so small," Ueta-san said.

"Then it's free?" my mom said brightly.

"Of course." Ueta-san nodded.

"But we didn't get any spoons for the soup," I remarked.

"It's meant to be drunk straight from the bowl." Ueta-san sat up even straighter and added, "Japanese-style."

How unusual that the Swiss, all the way over in Europe, living on mountainsides, drank their soup from bowls like the Japanese, while the Koreans, just a ferry ride away, used spoons! But Ueta-san had been in Canada longer than us, so he'd know these things.

"I like it," one of my sisters said, making slurping noises.

"Tasty but salty," my mom said.

"And thick," Ueta-san's wife said, smiling.

I sipped the hot liquid, agreeing.

Just then, our waitress, speed walking by our table on her way to the kitchen, skidded to a halt. "That's dipping sauce," she said flatly.

A sharp beak pecked in my stomach. We were doing something that made us stick out like sore, foreign thumbs.

"What is 'dipping sauce'?" Ueta-san sounded like an international exchange student asking for a definition in a spelling bee.

"You can dip your chicken in it or just pour it over your chicken. It's like gravy."

I was mortified that Chalet Farrah saw us drink gravy. She stood there like a schoolteacher, tapping a pen on her notepad, until we all put down our small white bowls. We picked up our knives and forks and started dipping the cut pieces of meat into what seconds ago had been Japanese-style soup.

At the nearest table, a middle-aged couple were desperately trying to stop their twitching mouths from stretching across their red faces.

"Delicious," my dad said, "Only one thing could make the chicken taste even better. Kimchi. We should have brought a jar."

Seriously? A jar of cabbage fermented with garlic, fish sauce, and hot spices opened in the middle of a Swiss restaurant? Within seconds, even the smoking section on the other side would smell the pungent odour, which could be pleasing only to those who had grown up eating kimchi. In her sensible shoes, Chalet Farrah would march over and make us put it away then command us to perform KP duties of washing dishes and peeling potatoes as punishment.

We picked the bones clean, ate every single fry and every crumb of the dinner rolls. There was zero wastage of our costly restaurant food. The waitress came with another seven white bowls. I stared down at my bowl, where a tiny piece of yellow lemon floated in the clear water. Chalet Farrah was about to tell us something, when a customer waving from another table caught her attention, and she walked away briskly, making a number-one sign behind her to indicate she was coming back.

"What's this?" my dad said.

Ueta-san gave a knowing nod. "It's lemonade."

My skin prickled. "We have soft drinks," I said.

"This lemonade is for cleansing the palate." He searched his mind for an example. "Like ginger after sushi." Before my mom could ask, he said, "Complimentary, free of charge."

Everyone else was satisfied with this answer, but something thrashed in my chest like a chicken grabbed for slaughter. I glanced over at the nearest table.

Horrified, I whispered, "Stop!"

With the bowls inches from their mouths, everyone froze like statues.

"It's *not* lemonade." I cocked my head to the next table.

The middle-aged couple, who I was certain were watching us with their peripheral vision, vigorously washed their fingers in their lemon water, as if they were surgeons prepping for surgery.

My sisters giggled, almost spilling their fragrant liquids, and the adults chorused, "Ohhh…" Everyone lowered the bowls and placed them back on the table.

Please, God, no more complimentary anything, I prayed.

Chalet Farrah rushed back to our table and seemed relieved to find us with our fingers in the lemon water.

When we exited the restaurant, the sun setting in the west was bright. Or maybe it seemed bright because we came out of a gravy-coloured interior. The seven of us packed into Ueta-san's sedan and retreated from the Swiss Chalet parking lot. I slumped in the back seat like an exhausted soldier in the trenches. With the windows rolled down, we drove down a busy road dotted with restaurants serving food from faraway countries.

"We should try a different restaurant, soon," Ueta-san said.

My dad said, "Let's remember to bring kimchi."

Lana Hall

///////////////

WE ARE ALL ANIMALS
AT NIGHT

I'll tell you a secret about working in a massage parlour: it's a lot of waiting around, usually late at night. We'd wait, half a dozen of us, in the dressing room as the evening wore on. On edge and exhausted in equal parts, we perched on the low-slung couch, adjusted the straps of our babydolls, listlessly fluffed our hair, ready to spring into action.

Girl, I'm going insane.

Oh please, I'm already there.

Then, we'd hear the front door open, the low murmur of a man's voice, the chirp of the receptionist from the parlour's reception desk. Some of us would circle the dressing-room door, ready in case he wanted to see the lineup, curious if he had booked someone specific. Then, the methodical thwack of the receptionist's pumps would sound down the long hallway as the girls swivelled towards her from their respective stations—pulling towels from the dryer, applying lipstick at the vanity, melting into the couch in a cloud of cigarettes and Pink Sugar perfume.

The receptionist would thrust four twenty-dollar bills into someone's hand; maybe mine, maybe not. "You're up. Sixty minutes in room four." For the rest of the girls, the night wore on, dark and still.

Honestly, that's most of working in a massage parlour: waiting around, wondering how much money you will—or won't—make on any given shift. I know, because I made my living that way for five years.

*

I was a university dropout in my early twenties when I started that gig, struggling to find my place in Toronto, a city where squalor and decadence collided behind the glass and steel of the downtown skyline. To get by, I took a job at a massage parlour in the northwest corner of the city, a place where factories stretched several blocks, separated by the odd strip mall full of nail salons, carpet dealers, banquet halls that morphed into after-hours clubs if you knew the right people. The garish yellow *M* of McDonald's arched high over everything, like a gateway to another world. Because of the way Toronto zoning bylaws work, most body-rub parlours are relegated to this part of the city, and after dark, "massage" signs wink and flash from almost every corner. *Finch Alley*, some people call it.

My regular shift at the parlour ran from 2 p.m. to 2 a.m., and I worked anywhere between three and six shifts a week, depending on how the cash was flowing. It was a job that was unbearably tangible at times, an onslaught of surgical scars and sun-damaged chests I rubbed oil over, the soft pallor of flesh under my hands that rarely saw the light of day. Yet it was also predicated on a precariously suspended reality, one I had to maintain with absolute precision to do my job well, to pretend that a profound mutual desire could be found for the low, low price of eighty dollars in a strip mall off a freeway. In real life I wouldn't dare be so giving. I can't say I was particularly good at any of this by the time 2 a.m. rolled around, makeup melting off my face, puffiness blooming under my eyes, a rapidly dwindling patience for the reassurance some men desperately sought: So, how was it for you?

The rabbit warren of hallways and thinly walled rooms felt insular at that hour, the click of stilettos on laminate less urgent than during the day. A dampness I always associated with the night shift hung in the air, mingling with the smell of smoke and coconut air freshener. Night shift did not discriminate, and the men who wandered in after dark were as varied as they come: they were travelling on business or headed home from factory shifts, students taking a break from all-nighters, bros on their way back from the bar. They were tall and short and young and old, of every race and cultural background imaginable. You could never predict who would come in, except to say with certainty that they would want a level of womanly validation I was simply too tired to give. Half-dressed and exhausted, I often didn't have the patience for their hands on me, the array of intimate requests they crept in seeking—touch me, kiss me, make me an entirely different world than the one outside these doors—when all I craved was the privacy of my own bed. My world outside the parlour was small—just a ground-floor apartment in midtown Toronto that looked out into an alley, while a radiator clanked and hissed at all hours of the night and day. But it was a place where my thoughts, and my body, were my own.

Despite the demands of the job, there was a stillness to the nights I found alluring. There was a poise to the velvety darkness of parking lots, the soft buzz of neon lights shaped like palm trees, as if they were also waiting at attention for the inevitable flurry of activity that punctuated those long periods of quiet. People's needs at 2 a.m. are equal parts fervent and fundamental, somehow stripped of all pretense by the cover of darkness. What do you need if you're out seeking services at night? Food, sex, shelter. The staunch of a wound. Being part of that felt like a reprieve from the day's complexities, a world which launched a steady barrage of information and demanded endless analyses, caring little for our overstimulated brains. The days were full of subway delays and deferred student-loan payments, of agonizing small talk and headlines about inflation.

At night we're just animals, I was reminded. The clients, yes, seeking release they couldn't admit during daylight hours, but also the workers who manned the various portions of the strip mall after dark. The way we cared for each other, sometimes more in silent gestures than anything else, felt connected to our deepest instincts as pack animals. No matter how much I wanted to go home, there was some comfort in the simplicity of that connection.

*

Memory has a way of smoothing jagged edges, leaving us with a haze of nostalgia that overlooks the most painful parts of our past lives, so I can't be sure how much I really miss the nights themselves and how much my brain is playing tricks on me. It defies logic that any part of me longs for the precarious earnings and long hours of massage-parlour work, the exhausting level of physical and emotional intimacy required, the shame that grew exponentially the farther away I slipped from what had once looked like a promising journalism career. However, I do know I miss the community it gave me membership to, the pack we inadvertently travelled in. I miss the silent language we developed, the way nothing was asked of me by other night-shift workers, the sense that I was enough just by showing up.

Cab drivers—who are also paid in cash and depend on volume for their livelihood—would pick me up at the end of shift and commiserate, rosary beads swinging from their rearview mirrors as we pulled onto dark freeways. How was work? Busy? They would ask. No, not really, I would say. You? As the cab whizzed down an eerily empty Gardiner Expressway, we'd laugh, try to unpack what made a slow shift or a busy one, what made people need us—or not. A dearth of sports games. The end of the month. Tax-refund season. Inertia. Once, a cab broke down in a snowstorm on the highway while taking me home, and the driver immediately phoned his friend, another driver, and gently walked me over to his cab, parked farther down the highway, when it arrived. Snow hurled sideways at us, my driver's tie flapping in the squall, his bare forearms braced against the cold. Get home safe, he told me, please.

At the twenty-four–seven coffee shop across the street from the parlour, women filled my Styrofoam cup, glancing wordlessly at the strip of bare skin between my coat and the tops of my stockings, but still making sure my cup was full to the top, passing me extra packets of sugar, sometimes a muffin from the day-old basket. Kids in their early twenties manned the counter at all-night fast-food joints, where I'd go between clients on slow shifts, needing something to wake up my neurons: salt, heat, grease. The shock of cold air on my legs at midnight. We knew so little about each other's lives—how could we?—but forced into this strange cohort of ragged work hours, I felt we sometimes shared a look of recognition: of people whittling time away as we tended to the incessant hungers of others.

*

When I finally did leave the sex trade, after finishing my bachelor's degree as a mature student, I spent seven years working in "good" jobs in the corporate sector. This meant, as I understood it, that I didn't work nights, that I was a salaried employee, and that I had dental benefits. I had a shiny access card that opened doors—to a gleaming, marble elevator bank, to planters full of plastic ferns, to blocks of cubicles illuminated by fluorescent lighting, a land of perpetual daytime.

Unlike sex work, my "good" jobs didn't threaten to overthrow traditional power structures. Many sex workers, including myself, have long hypothesized that the reason so many people in power work to keep the commercial sex trade marginalized is because they're threatened by it—by the idea that it's the only field where women outearn men, that it's an industry where women get to call the shots, and that women profit off something that men have been told they're entitled to for free: sex and attention in equal parts. In my experience of the corporate landscape, there was none of this radical power structure, only an upholding of the traditional: men talking and women listening, men in powerful positions getting both credit and profit for the labour of women beneath them. Is this what I worked so hard for? I wondered daily.

As I moved through this new world, merging into the throng of daytime professionals that swelled throughout the downtown core, absorbed by their smartphone screens, and proffering the barest morsels of small talk, I felt little of the camaraderie I once did while working night shifts. I'm unsure why I felt this dissonance, and it occurs to me now that it could have been more self-imposed than anything. Perhaps my experience in the parlours of Finch Alley felt so removed from what I perceived as the experience of my corporate colleagues and their "good life choices" that I created that distance myself, imposter syndrome as thick as the steam that rose from the downtown subway grates during the winter. When I was assigned a crisis communications task, which was often part of my job, I would try to cheer myself up by silently joking that after everything, my livelihood somehow still depended on men employing bad judgment. But there was nobody around who would understand, so the joke fell flat, even in my head.

Sometimes when I headed home from the office, stuffed onto a packed streetcar, I remembered nights when our strip mall felt like a kingdom, where we scurried from block to block like savvy woodland creatures, coats zipped over our lingerie, faces alight under the weak yellow streetlamps, dispatching coffee orders or supplies from clerks at the late-night convenience stores. Condoms. Baby oil. Hot Cheetos. "We know where she works," their faces said, but it felt less like a judgment and more like an acknowledgement. We were in it together; an ecosystem of tending to each other's needs, brazen and intimate at the same time.

Once I sat on the leather couch in the dressing room, which was just an extension built onto the massage parlour that housed an industrial-sized washer and dryer, a makeup table, and a precarious utility shelf crammed with supplies: towels, mineral oil, rubbing alcohol, Kleenex. Nursing a black tea, I steeled myself before my last appointment of the night. It was booked as an hour-long shower session, which I hated. Sixty minutes with a regular who would never say a word to me, who just wanted to touch my breasts as we slowly turned to prunes under the tepid water, while I tried to make each stifled yawn look like it was, in fact, a shiver of ecstasy. "I don't know if I can make it," I said, half joking but half imploring the five other girls who sat wedged on the couch with me, or sprawled on threadbare Ikea chairs.

"Baby, come sit by me," said Cheryl, an attendant from Newfoundland in her early fifties with sun-crinkled skin the colour of almonds and a voice like gravel. I plodded over to where she sat at the makeup table and pulled up a stool.

"At least let me fix your hair," she said. I complied.

Cheryl brushed my hair extensions out with her fingers, acrylic nails flashing, pink as Malibu. Then she took out a wide-barrel curling iron and meticulously worked my unruly hair into waves, smiling and humming periodically at her handiwork. "There," she said when she was finished. "So pretty."

I felt so much care in that moment I could barely breathe, and it occurred to me that I'd never had a woman, before or since, handle my hair so tenderly.

Once, the fire alarm went off in the office tower where I worked downtown. We crammed into the stairwell, lurching down dozens of flights. It was the most unscripted moment I had encountered since starting that office job and for a moment I marvelled at the chaos of it all: the unvarnished panic and confusion on people's faces, the small gesture of kindness when I dropped my elevator card and someone picked it up for me. Maybe this is it, I thought. Maybe this is when the adrenaline and uncertainty give way to something more human, where we seek relief in collective company. Maybe we'll all go out for a drink and watch the fire trucks tend to the real emergency. But when the final door banged open on ground level, spitting us out into the alley behind a steakhouse, everyone dispersed in separate directions, scattering as far as the eye could see.

*

Last year, New York mayor Eric Adams was quoted referring to cooks, fast-food workers, dishwashers, and messengers as "low-skill workers," proclaiming they simply don't have the skills to "sit in a corner office." Like Toronto, New York relies on a variety of minimum-wage and night-shift workers to keep its culture "vibrant"—a term often used in city-building and real estate circles—or at least convenient. In fact, according to the Bureau of Labor Statistics, more than fifteen million Americans work night shifts. In Canada, it's closer to 1.8 million, or 12 percent of the working population. Could not a single one of those people have the "skills" to work in a corner office? When I read Adams's quote, I was back, for the briefest of seconds, in that dark parking lot under a red-lit "massage" sign, watching the outline of a coffee-shop server across the street as she wiped down the midnight counter, over and over. I thought of her thankless work and the comfort she provided to so many people moving through that transient space, the way she may have wanted to do something—anything—else with her time, but perhaps was not afforded the opportunity. What a world, in which her labour went unvalued, perhaps unnoticed altogether.

Adams's comments ricocheted through social media for months, at one point resulting in a tweet about how most corner-office professionals wouldn't be able to handle even one overnight shift at Waffle House. But Adams isn't alone in his simplistic view; many of the jobs that require overnight shifts are considered "low-skill" roles by those in power, regardless of how essential they might be. How quickly the discourse moves from "frontline workers" to "low-skilled labourers" as soon as the concepts of unions or minimum-wage increase make an appearance. This idea of night-shift jobs being less desirable, work people do because they "have to," not because they want to, is true sometimes. It was obvious to me that many in my night-shift network were working gigs as a stopgap on the way to something else, but to me that never made any of us less deserving. In reality, I thought of us as some of the strongest, the most resourceful, the most skilled at defusing confrontations that often come with late-night interactions.

"You're better than this job," clients sometimes said to me while I was working nights. Often they'd say it in the awkward and delicate moments immediately after a session, as we towelled off together and I stripped the massage table—moments where men were often fraught with shame, resignation, and satiation in equal parts, and words tumbled clumsily from their mouths. They meant it as a compliment, but it was a sentiment I hated. *You're better than this.* As though somewhere, there was a woman who wasn't.

I've seen security guards defuse a knife fight. I once watched a fast-food server placate a violent customer with nothing more than her voice and a stale honey cruller at her disposal. I've met few professionals since who, I think, could handle those wearying hours, and even fewer who could still react with tact and effectiveness under pressure, especially considering the low, precarious wages these gigs often pay. Plus, there's a danger to working jobs with these hours and demands on a long-term basis. Statistics have long shown that people who work night shifts are more likely to battle stress, illness, even premature death. Whether those late-night needs—for food, for sex—are real or perceived, as long as there's a demand, profit-driven businesses will want to capitalize on it, perhaps at the very expense of the workers who take those shifts. The price we pay to keep cities thrumming and hungers satiated at all hours of the night and day is steep.

*

It's been years since I held a job requiring those kinds of late-night shifts. I woke recently at exactly 2 a.m., as I often do, pulled from slumber by some unnameable cue. I poured a glass of water and stood at my apartment window, suspended high above a ribbon of expressway. From behind the glass, everything was hushed at that hour. Then I reminded myself that an entire eco-system still hums and clanks and keeps the world stitched together quietly: the municipal salt truck scattering brine down the street. The yellow sign of the twenty-four–seven grocery down the block advertising milk, bread, cigarettes. The wink of a red taillight as it trails across the expressway and flashes out of sight. I can't, of course, know who it might be; perhaps another aimless man not ready to go home yet, rootless and restless and looking for validation in all the wrong places; perhaps another night-shift worker on her way home, forming an unspoken understanding with her cab driver. Sometimes I think I have nothing to show for those years spent tending to people's needs after hours, a period of my life as brief and transient as the red glow of that receding taillight. But I know the stories of the city after dark, and I keep those with me, always.

Ariel Gordon

////////////

ROTTEN

Result: High grade squamous intraepithelial lesion. What it means: Moderate to severe abnormal changes were seen. This result is more serious. What you should do: Make sure your health care provider has made a colposcopy appointment for you.

—*What You Need to Know about Preventing Cervical Cancer*, CervixCheck, CancerCare Manitoba.

Q: How do I recognize if my tree is infected?
A: Look into the tree canopy, wilting of leaves is usually the first stage of DED, followed by yellowing then browning of the leaves. If you are unsure please call 311 for a Forestry Technician to inspect.

—*Frequently Asked Questions: Dutch Elm Disease*, Urban Forestry, City of Winnipeg

July 2021. Evening. I heatwave-sit on my front steps, hoping to catch a stray breeze, legs folded over my cervix, a rotten egg I cradle in my lightly-used loins—thousands of gametes, one child—for fear of breaking it.

Duds are like bombs, their terrible smell, their blossoming rot just barely contained by their shells. I know my cervix isn't a dud or even a booby trap, but I still I clench like I have an aching bladder-full, like I'm about to Frankenstein up the stairs to the only bathroom, only to find that someone is already using it, firmly installed.

Fifteen feet away, my hundred-year-old boulevard elm is glorious, full of sap and leaves that reach over the house, the dense spread of three stories. It has scars on its trunk from generations of snow- and earth-moving machines, leftover nails and industrial staples from years of tree-banding, abandoned now. Best-practices.

In May and June some years, worms hang from its bare branches over the front door, wriggling across the screens greenly, investigating the mailbox.

I sit on the stairs with my rotten cervix, my sexually transmitted angst, and watch the tree move and not move. We not-move together. I have watched the cats nibble on the crabgrass at the elm's base, chase the white moths the worms become in the dry grass at twilight. I have pulled insistent dandelions from amongst its surface roots. My neighbours mow my stretch of boulevard grass now without even asking when they do theirs, a shared obligation, the unsharp blades of my push mower, clenched, silent as my rotten cervix. Once, a wheel fell off my push mower mid-push—a failed contraction, the labour nurse / my gas-powered neighbour muttering encouragement, insistent.

I will have to call to get the biopsy result today. To summon Urban Forestry technicians to stare up at a flagging branch, to decide whether the tree gets the neon orange dot of a Dutch elm disease diagnosis, of death, the hiss of the spray paint like an inadvertent intake of breath over the phone, the results in.

I don't know what—

*

My ladyparts hate me but the view from the sixth floor of the Manitoba Clinic—which houses neat rows of OB/GYNs, like rows of incubators in old-timey movies—saves me every time.

Heavy menstrual bleeding, almost hemorrhagic? *Window.* Fluid-filled cyst the size of a mandarin orange on an ovary? *Window.*

The view is all gleaming asphalt and a rising river of old trees, swamping downtown. I am reassured that the city vanishes under the canopy in summer.

Today is my colposcopy, and somehow, the window isn't enough of an intervention—I find myself pacing the pregnant hallway, walking my suspect cervix like a pissy dog on a leash. I stop and look down to the fifth-floor balcony, where the planters are filled with bamboo stakes and plastic-owl facades, pointed in all the cardinal directions.

My cervix and I are amused by the hardcore pigeon deterrence (or HPD), and then I spot a plastic wolf the size of a late-summer zucchini, tucked in amongst the bamboo, which looks to be half boar and, also, enraged about being so small.

For most of the spring and summer, I have been owl watching in a cemetery, from an hour or so before sundown until it gets fully dark and the owls emerge from their snoozing roosts and begin their day. We go in the hopes of seeing the best bits of the great horned owl lifecycle so I can write a book about it or maybe just a brochure. I have been admiring shed owl feathers but return them to the ground after I've photographed them, after I've turned them this way and that in what's left of the light, filled with admiration. Legally, you can't own owl feathers, but ejecta is another matter, so I have a Ziploc bag of owl pellets that I'm saving for winter like a taxidermist's advent calendar. But I haven't owl-watched in weeks now and miss spending my Saturday nights sundowning with a GHOW pair that refused to nest, this year's legacy only pellets and shed feathers. This year's activity was only me, watching owls fly away.

Lying on the exam table, I hear my gyne say, "The thing on my head is a microscope."

"I can't see you," I say, "but I believe you."

Today, she is taking a tissue sample, to test for cervical cancer. I busy myself visualizing dwarf wolves prowling windowsills instead of human papillomavirus (or HPV) lesions on my cervix. (I have already thoroughly visualized the lesions as black, like the lichen that specializes in rocky slopes in Shield country. My favourite thing in high summer when I was younger was the crunch when the dried-out lichen was stepped on....) This summer, I have a dwarf Saskatoon manufacturing purple in a pot on my balcony. Maybe the wolf would feel drawn to it, feel a miniaturized kinship?

I say, out loud, that I once made out with a boy with cold sores.

"My tongue and gums got super swollen afterwards," I elaborate. "I thought all my teeth were going to fall out."

The gyne says that's herpes simplex virus (or HSV), which, of course, I know. She mentions that she might perform a loop electrosurgical excision procedure (or LEEP) on my cervix later, to remove the infected tissue. The brochure, tucked in my bag as I walk away from the building, also mentions cryosurgery, which

I felt I should request on principle, so my cervix can be bionic or preserved in a vat next to Steve Job's head, nevermind the cruelty of watery discharge for weeks.

These are the jokes I should have deployed in the gyne's office, like sexually transmitted diseases, but instead I felt tired and sad, and now I am trapped in my car by rain. For the first time in my life, I am thrilled when it rains.

Sitting there, I remember that when the gyne said, "Your cervix is shaped like a donut," I wanted to ask what kind.

If I could choose, I'd want my cervix to resemble a cruller.

*

Coming out in the evening, looking for a moment of green transport—like a pelican's shadow at the river's edge, covering me entirely for a moment, like wading out in a lake and finally making it up to my armpits, my water-wing breasts vanishing under the swells—except spotting the flagging leaves on a branch up high.

The branch is nearest the road, overhanging my dirty little Prius, the leaves obviously dry and crisp, even from here. My stomach and my rotten cervix clench.

What could I have done to prevent this? Heat-wave watering? Preventative insecticide injections? Paying for treatment out of my rotten poetry budget? Or was it inevitable, an aging tree, an infected city, and my hippy-dippy neighbourhood one of the hardest hit? But this is not the urban forest, or an illustration of the three hundred thousand elms that have survived our civic imagination, our settler demands; it is *my* tree, my beloved, still strong but showing weakness seventy-five feet up—shrieking merlin height. Street lamp height, even with dreadful full-moon

LEDs. (Like a forehead microscope focused on my diseased ladyparts, the light is unflinching.)

I have no symptoms, no phantom ache, but according to CancerCare I missed my test twice over, all the safeguards and bookkeeping failing me and my cervix. I should have known, somehow. Or I should have been out, merrily sharing my STI.

The gyne said HPV has been having a party on my cervix, and here's me with anxiety that no one will show up at my book launches. Except I didn't have to send out a single invite. The gyne said it's proof that I had sex at some point in my life. Except the infection didn't resolve, like a twenty-year-old fling, like an old elm brooding over a trunk full of elm bark beetles, each of them wreathed with sticky fungal spores, anticipating a threesome with revving chainsaws.

Oh God. I hate waiting for test results. For authorities to tell you what's next, your diagnosis just another piece of paper in a file in a row of file cabinets. I want an elaborate chart of my sadness. Stage-four sadness—all over my flagging face and in my pants.

*

That night, watching the rain pour down—a month's worth of rain in one day, like a basin that has been kicked over—I couldn't dredge up the energy to run to the house.

But I didn't want to sit in the car forever, so I opened the car door and took two steps and stood next to—and then leaned on—the trunk of my boulevard elm.

A mature elm might be umbrella-shaped, but it isn't an umbrella, so rain made its way through the branches, the flagging leaves, and landed on my head and shoulders. I was getting increasingly wet.

But the space under the branches, between my car and the house, felt like a spare room someone I trusted was offering me. So, I put my lined forehead against the rough trunk and focused on breathing, listening to the pelting rain and my breath.

*

I don't know what—

I don't know what to do with my climate-changed heat stress, years of drought shelved alongside this year's heat dome. Instagram is all aluminum foil-covered windows, the forests to the east and west burning. The smoke hasn't drifted into town yet. The tree hasn't been condemned. But it's coming.

I dream of rain, scan the weather report full of headlines I don't want to read: extreme heat warnings, air quality warnings, empty farm dugouts, grasshopper infestations.

I haven't been dealing well with the heat. My house is not designed for weeks of high heat, rooms hot-air ballooning across airless afternoons. We retreat to our bedrooms, the window air conditioners/my mind whirring. We are heat-exhausted, hydro-affected, and I don't know what I'll do if my boulevard tree comes down.

What if the biggest loss in my life isn't my little granny, my divided father, his nose wandering across generations of angry women, but that elm? I would trade my mossy roof, my rotten cervix, for another leafy decade with that tree.

But maybe we don't get to choose. Maybe life isn't picking which catastrophe falls on your head—like a dead branch, like a super-storm's worth of rain.

Maybe life is just standing as close as you can to a tree. Feeling connected to the world, for however long you've both got.

Vance Wright

//////////////

BIRTH STORIES, ADOPTION, AND MYTHS

Imagine learning the word "adoption" at the same time you learn words like "mother," "father," "home," "birth," or "safe." Other words you learn are "abandoned," "given up," "loved," "wanted," and "adopted." You learn that the one who gave birth to you and your twin is a parent, that you have a mother, but that she gave you both up. You learn that the people looking after you are also your parents, a mother and father, who took in you and your twin. You are not related to your parents, but you are. They could not have babies of their own, so they adopted the two of you. You are told your biological mother wanted to keep you and your twin but couldn't because she was too young. You are told that she loved both of you, and that you and your twin were wanted, yet you know the two of you were still given up. You must reconcile the fact that you have no power to choose for yourself, that these people you find yourself with are your parents, and that you may never fully know who or where you came from. You don't remember a time where you weren't told any of this.

—Did you meet my father at a New Years Eve party?

—Yes!... How did you know that?

—Well,... We were born on September 1st, so if we count back nine months of pregnancy... that brings us to roughly Christmas to New Years.

—Ha ha ha, well, you were also premature, but your deduction isn't wrong.

Your father and I always wanted kids. We tried many times but God never sent us any that stayed. One afternoon, Grandma called us from Kamloops, saying that she had met a girl named Dawn-Marie who had a baby in her tummy, and was putting the baby up for adoption. She asked "are you interested?" so we packed our things into the car and zoooooomed up to Kamloops to meet her.

My earliest memory is being two or three years old; I am on a bed in a beige bedroom, and my tiny hands are holding a large storybook. My adoptive parents are reading to me, telling me the story of a fictional character who was adopted. The story was structured around the child wondering where they came from—what their birth story was. An image that has stayed with me is the child's face poking out of a vending machine where chocolate bars or Skittles would fall. A reader might wonder if they came from a baby-dispensing machine after their new parents had shoved some quarters into the coin slot.

I remember feeling strangely about this depiction, both repelled and taken in by its gravity. My adoptive parents (Bob and Teresa) had raised us from the beginning with a picture of our birth mother, and her name (Dawn-Marie), but there was always a sense of the mystical about her—a present absence, not a ghost but not quite fully coherent as a person either. While I knew I was brought into this world by her, I still felt this feeling of not quite knowing where I came from and how I had come into this world. Our birth story was repeated throughout our early life, especially before meeting our birth mother, but it still didn't feel quite real and never answered the question in the back of my mind.

Narratively, a birth comes either at the beginning or end of a story, punctuating either events being set in motion or coming to a close. Parents have their happily ever after, and a new hero is brought into their journey. Simba in *The Lion King* champions the hero's birth story, being lifted towards the sky on top of Pride Rock, in front of all the Animal Kingdom subjects. Birth is rarely figured as a transformative disruption that happens in the middle of the story, a volta. But this is what it felt like to me, being an adopted child, that my life was beginning in the middle of other people's stories, that there was a big universe out there that I was a small part of and had little control over.

Very early on, I was always aware that our birth story operated on multiple levels. It was constructed to help my twin and me feel secure in being adopted, that we were loved and wanted despite being given up. It also functioned as a litany of reassurance for them too, I suspect, as parents who are not biologically related to their children. I always wondered what story Dawn-Marie told herself about her pregnancy and our birth, and I hoped she felt secure too. Throughout my life, there always seemed to be a tension within our entire family. I knew I would never say to them, "You're not my real parents!" because I was acutely aware of the effect it would have. It was also a phrase I vowed I would never say to my birth mother.

In a way, our birth story was a mythic speech act, where everything within the confines of its narrative had come to signify multiple things, referential squared, or even cubed. It wasn't so much about the birth itself, but rather everything surrounding the birth, the paperwork, the relationships, the transition from people to parents, and a girl to a mother to a birth parent. If the birth story was about the birth itself, it would probably be a grisly narrative.

I was standing in the kitchen when my water broke. It was eight-thirty or nine at night, and I had to get Grandpa Barry and Grandma Yvonne to drive me to the hospital. When my contractions sped up and I was actually in labour, a foot came out first and your heartbeat began to disappear from the monitor. We think the umbilical cord was wrapped around your neck. The doctor quickly transitioned to a C-section, and retrieved you first before getting your sibling. You were taken out at 10:01 p.m., and your twin came out at 10:02 p.m. I woke up much later, and the nurses put you both in my arms and I cried.

When we met Dawn-Marie, she asked us, "Do you want this baby?" We said, "Yes, we do." Dawn-Marie said, "I will think on it." We drove back to Nelson. Months go by, and then we get a call from Dawn-Marie, saying, "I'm having twins, do you want these babies?" and we said, "Yes, we do." Dawn-Marie said, "I will think on it. Come up to Kamloops." So, we packed our things into the car and zooooomed up to Kamloops again.

Adoption is a process which structurally severs and forges families. The state separates children from their biological parents in order for them to be given to their adoptive parents. In both open and closed adoptions, the adoptive parents usually have more control and power as to how the adoption will unfold, if at all. The adoptive parents are able to tell any story they wish about the origins of the child they adopt, and the birth mother is usually counted lucky by society if she is included. Many adoptees do not find out about their adoption until much later in life, sometimes not at all. The state has used the process of adoption as another mode of disrupting cultural transference between generations of Indigenous people, alongside and after the residential schools, another way of "saving the child while killing the Indian." In the eyes of the state, nurture should and would override nature.

I eventually met my birth mother, at the age of five, at the Vancouver Aquarium in Stanley Park. I vividly remember standing out front, posing with all three adults and my twin in the rain, the Orca statue behind us. While five years passes quickly for me now, the period before I knew her feels disproportionately long in my mind. During those first five years, my parents tried their best to make sure my twin and I grew up with secure attachments—with varying results, which are no fault of theirs. A frequent story that was told was our birth story. We would ask for it repeatedly, I think due to the many questions we had, but with no way to frame them into language yet. Again, this story contained some answers but not all of them—something I have come to realize defines the experience of adoption. Adoption is a process, an experience, a practice, that resists neat narratives, genres, and stable categorizations.

It was after this first meeting that I noticed my parents started to trace features of our appearance and behaviour to our bio-logical mother. This seemed strange to me because it wasn't part of our conversations before we met her, only after. I began to wonder if my parents were also insecure about the way our family structure was forged. Strange thoughts for a five-year-old to be having, realising that all your parents are people, wonder-ing if your biological mom was tracing features and behaviours back to herself, or to your adoptive parents. I wondered if her experience being adopted to a white family was similar to mine.

Later in life, during college, I began learning about the Sixties Scoop—about how Indian Agents would steal children from com-munities, from hospital beds, and adopt them out to white families. The intent was to "kill the Indian and save the child." It was their aim to stop the transmission of culture that happens within a Native family and begin socializing native kids as white by white parents. During lecture, I drifted off into memory, recalling being a child and saying to my adoptive mom, "I wish my skin was light like yours. Kids say I'm dirty because my skin is brown." Her response was that she wished she was tan like me year-round, and it half consoled me. Another memory comes up of my twin and me at the beach, running in the water and then rolling in the white sand while we were still wet, to try and see what it felt like to fit in, to not be visible in a town that has less than 1 percent of a BIPOC (Black, Indigenous, and people of colour) population. Seeing the ways white supremacy was steeped inside of me lit a fire in me to burn these internalized ideas out of myself whenever I came across them.

I remember the first time we met. We had spent the day at the Vancouver aquarium, you were dressed in your cute

little rain jacket running with sneakered feet through the various tanks and displays, surprise and curiosity on your face. We walked to the seawall after, and you were holding my hand when I began crying. You looked up at me and asked "Why are you crying, Dawn-Marie?" I crouched down beside you and looked you in the eyes and I said "I was so scared that you wouldn't love me." Your little five-year-old hand reached up to hold my wet cheek and you said "Of course I love you, you're my birth mom."

My twin and I loved *Hercules,* a movie that came out in 1997, the year we met Dawn-Marie. In the movie, Hercules is told he was abandoned, and his adoptive parents raised him thinking he was a gift from the Gods. This tale paralleled the story we had been told of our birth and adoption. Hercules seeks answers to his origins and realizes his grand hero's journey of reconnecting with his godly family, with fame and fortune and all its trappings. His parents lose speaking roles after he leaves home, replaced by his birth parents speaking throughout the entire film.

As we grew older, Dawn-Marie would visit every summer or so, and we began to hear other narratives surrounding our birth—that she had met our biological father at a party; that he had taken off when he found out she was pregnant and giving birth to the children; that she loved us deeply but at the age of nineteen couldn't keep us, that giving us up was the hardest thing she had ever done. This answered some questions, but also raised others.

In 2002, *Lilo & Stitch* came out. As nine-year-olds, we were still excited about Disney films, and I remember crying in the theatre but not knowing why. Looking back, it was a very different story about family and adoption from *Hercules.* An Indigenous Hawaiian family is mourning the loss of two parents and resisting the state in further severing the family. A pet-turned-extra-kid puts further stress on the family, but ultimately proves that the plastic nature of kinship can not only resist state separation but also has the capacity to envelop new members during crisis. No family member gets left behind.

> Dawn-Marie asked us, "Will you love these babies?" and we said, "Yes, we will." "Okay," she said. "You can have these babies." Oh, we felt so lucky and happy!! We drive back down to Nelson. Months go by, and then we get a call saying, "The twins are coming, the twins are coming!" So, we packed up the car and zooooomed up to Kamloops AGAIN. On September 1st, 1992, you and your sibling came into the world. You didn't want to come out, so the doctors had to open up her belly and get you. The nurses brought you to us, and we counted to make sure you had ten little fingers and ten little toes, and you DID have ten little fingers and ten little toes.

Puberty is a transition for everyone. When I began puberty, the narrative of our adoption shifted from our birth to our genes, the adults surrounding us trying to nail down exactly what was *Nature* in us, with no real interest in pinning down what was *Nurtured*. Every aspect of how I looked and acted was traced in some way to Dawn-Marie. I was the signifier, a child shifting into something else. What was familiar about me as a child was defamiliarized in my pubescent body, I was constantly signifying to my parents that I was not of their body. The shape of my foot, the sound of my laugh, my short temper, my skin-stretching growth spurts.

This made me deeply insecure about my body. I thought I was just me, that it didn't matter if a certain part of it was nature or nurture—desperate, as most teenagers are, to be autonomous and define yourself on your own terms. I feel differently about it now. As the tectonics of my body seemed to cool, and I began to settle into teenage angst. I remember hearing about twin and triplet adoption studies, where twins or triplets were separated at birth and raised in completely different towns but would grow up to live similar lives—down to driving the same brands of cars, dating similar people, and eating similar things. Not only did this perturb me as overly deterministic and vaguely eugenicist, it made me start to question the ethics of adoption at its core. Is it ethical to raise a child in a way that is so radically different from their peers? Is it more ethical to sever families than to change the systems that produce inequalities that then create the need to sever families? What stories are ethical to tell an adopted child, and what are the long-term effects of them?

Around this time, Angelina Jolie was adopting children from her travels. Adoption seemed to be everywhere, and peers at school would draw parallels between what the stars were doing and my family structure. I didn't know what intersectionality was at the time, nor who Gayatri Spivak was, but I could plainly see how power pervades the system of adoption, of "white women saving brown women from brown men." At no point did the stories of Jolie's adoptions centre the birth mothers of these adopted children, possibly for safety or security reasons, but instead they dwelled on Jolie's (apparent) purity and kindness. How brave she was, and how moral she was, to raise these brown children alongside her white, biological children and love them just the same. This epic performance of adoptive and mixed family life in LA spelled out to me the way power moves through adoption. The adopting parents are necessarily more empowered than the birth mother. It is not a cheap process. There are legal fees, there are checks and balances in the agreement, regardless of whether the adoption is open or closed.

Luckily, Dawn-Marie had a lot of control in how the adoption went. It was an anomaly that my parents were willing to have a closed adoption on her account and asked to open it up as we grew older. Both of my mothers refer to each other as my mom, which I count myself lucky for. But my peers still perceived my adoption in certain ways—calling me a "true bastard" because I was born out of wedlock, that I had been "saved from poor living conditions." When telling our birth story on a public stage, we signify the purity of our white parents and the imposed shame or inadequacy of our brown parents. Instead, we speak of the charity and goodwill of settlers, while our disconnection to our origin is erased. We signify the pain our birth parents face in having us and giving us up. We signify the fulfillment of our adoptive parents' dream to have children. We signify the state's ugly intent, and unending love of our origins.

Also absent from the narratives are the number of children in care here on Turtle Island who cannot or would not be adopted, another way in which the separation of families has always been violent. Everyone wants to adopt the tabula rasa that is a newborn baby, or perhaps the perfect orphan who is sad but ultimately just wants to be loved, like Annie. Narratives of adoption and foster care do not leave space for messiness, for dealing with the trauma that the very system itself instills in those who go through it. Annie never acts out and breaks plates or intentionally scrapes her knee or inflicts pain onto small creatures as a way of exerting control in a world where children have none. However, these are things I, and other adopted or fostered individuals I know, have done before. These reactions seem logical to me, growing up in the confusion and messiness of adopted life.

Adoption defies stable categories, as I love all my parents, while also being keenly aware of the ways in which it has been used by the state to disrupt and attempt to end cultural practices of Indigenous cultures across Turtle Island. I do not count myself as part of the Millennial Scoop, but my adoption produced the same results; because my mother was scooped, and I was adopted, we were not able to grow up in community, practicing our culture. If she hadn't been scooped, I would not have been born, but at least any child she might have had would have been connected in a way I still am yearning for. This is not to say I wish my life had been different, or that my birth mother's life had been different, but that it was beyond my control. What is in my control is how I talk about this history. Adoption severs and forges, it gives and it takes away, it is both secure and insecure, socially and politically concerned with issues of nature and nurture, neither of which are just progressive, liberal, or conservative. It is an ending, a beginning, and a middle.

We drove back down to Nelson, and everyone was So Excited to have both of you home. We drove up, Up, UP! the mountain to the lab and showed you to our friends Judy and Tim, and Jill and David, and Tina and Dave. We drove down, Down, DOWN! the mountain and you two met Grandma Ruby for the first time. You puked all down her back as she held you.

James Cairns

MY STRUGGLE
AND "MY STRUGGLE"

I might have had a mid-life crisis without realizing it at the time. In my late thirties, over a span of two years, I pledged enduring love to three different women. I moved houses and cities multiple times, fell off the wagon, and prepared to quit my job so I could move to the other side of the world. I thought I was doing just fine.

According to Elliott Jaques, the Canadian psychoanalyst who coined the term "mid-life crisis" in 1957, we're prone to "rapid transition" in our late thirties because, for the first time, we face "the reality and inevitability of one's own eventual personal death." Even young children understand death at an abstract level. But, long into adulthood, most people repress the enormity of the fact that they will die.

By our mid-thirties, the reality of death is no longer easily avoided. Our parents' health declines; they die. Our bodies show the first signs of irreversible decay. The early thrill of marriage and parenthood fades. Careers grow stale. Big plans wither. It's a decisive moment—a crisis—in the life course.

How to respond to this new world, in which death—both real and symbolic—looms large? Fall to pieces, seize up, kill yourself? "Breakdown may be avoided," suggests Jaques, "by means of strengthening manic defences." Buying a sports car, leaving your wife for your secretary—classic mid-life–crisis stuff. There's also the possibility of resolving the crisis by integrating mortality's dark truth in a fuller life. Jaques points to Dickens and Shakespeare turning to more "tragic and philosophical content" later in their careers, as compared to the "lyrical and descriptive content" of their youth.

The autumn in which I turned thirty-seven, death wasn't much on my mind. I didn't feel old or think much about aging. I had all my hair. I was unmarried and childless. I was on my first sabbatical from teaching, living in Brooklyn, and writing a book. My partner was making a film. Each morning, I biked past brownstones and junkyards en route to a shared writers' space.

In November, I fell in love with a writer. In January, I left my partner. As I packed books into boxes in our sublet, she asked if I'd lost my mind. I listened to her words, but trusted my reason. I was following my destiny.

My new relationship lasted five months. One sunny morning, after playing tennis, I told the writer I'd fallen in love with that I didn't love her anymore. I still loved my ex and wanted to try again with her.

My ex didn't reject the idea, but couldn't start in earnest before moving past the pain I'd caused. So began a year of being together but not being together.

Alone in my apartment back in Canada that fall, I sat on a velour easy chair and read the first five volumes of Karl Ove Knausgaard's 3,500-page autobiographical novel, *My Struggle*. I'd long avoided the book, repulsed by the author's apparent self-absorption and titular reference to Hitler's memoir-manifesto. But while driving through the Adirondacks to visit my ex (or, not-ex?), I heard Knausgaard interviewed on the radio and became intrigued by his project. Before finishing ten pages, I was obsessed with his story and his way of telling it.

That fall, I read Knausgaard every night after jogging. Most days, on campus, I read pages between student meetings. I read Knausgaard while watching Trump's election win. I read Knausgaard while refusing to consider the possibility that I might have feelings for a graduate student. *My Struggle* was the most stable part of my life.

Was I going through a mid-life crisis? You laugh. But I'm hesitant to apply the label to my experience because I didn't think about it that way at the time. Crises involve real-world events *and* interpretations of those events. Situations on their own, apart from how we define them, are simply that: situations. I saw plainly the dramatic swings in my life; I just didn't view them as adding up to a crisis.

My most rational, fully conscious thoughts during that period didn't explore common mid-life stressors. Not once in my internal dialogues about my disruptive behaviour did I think in terms of life transitions or milestones. Not in chats with friends, not in therapy sessions. Today, I shake my head while recalling the self-narrative I performed at that time because so much of it consisted of lies.

I lied about my affairs. Lied about my drinking. Lied about my confidence in this or that decision. I told truths, too. But truth was mixed with fears and wishes, and the compulsion to manage others' impressions of me.

Was I ever fully honest and consistent while moving through years of deceit and turmoil?

My devotion to Knausgaard was pure. I spent months sitting with *My Struggle*, looking forward to getting back to it, and reflecting on its pages. What so captivated me?

In the *New Yorker*, James Wood says *My Struggle* is a book about death. Obviously, the death of the author's father drives the narrative. However, Wood argues: "the more pervasive struggle is with death itself, in which writing is both weapon and battlefield. Writing promises to rescue moments from the march of time, but serious writing also lays bare, examines, dramatizes—and, in this sense, seems to prolong—that death journey."

Poet and novelist Ben Lerner says Knausgaard writes as though "everything seems equally worthy of differentiation"— memories of comic books, sunsets, and forest smells; the virtue of soft versus crunchy cornflakes; the feeling of falling in love; hours of cleaning up after a dead man; masturbating; writing; not-writing; making tea. If mortality is *My Struggle*'s main character, the book's glacial pace and obsessive attention to detail are acts of rebellion against death.

Only recently, at forty-two, while thinking about what our literary obsessions reveal, did I see in those tumultuous years my preoccupation with death. If you'd asked me at the time, I would have told you I didn't think about my youth ending, my going "over the hill," my dying. My obsession with *My Struggle* tells a different story.

Reconceiving of those years in terms of mid-life crisis doesn't absolve me of responsibility for the harm I caused then (nor am I suggesting that everything I did is regrettable). Rather, the lens of mid-life crisis reveals logic (however flawed) in a period of my life that once seemed largely incomprehensible. I wouldn't have grasped that logic, or learned from it, if I hadn't reflected on why I was so enchanted by Knausgaard's book.

You might want to ask yourself about your searing passion for the Toronto Raptors. Or reflect on what you get, besides flowers, from obsessive gardening. Or maybe it doesn't work that way. Maybe the secrets of our fixations are recoverable only in retrospect. In any case, the complexity of lives, in crisis or not, is best understood when we examine indirect expressions of thought and feeling. In the words of artist Amy Krouse Rosenthal, who died at fifty-one: "Pay attention to what you pay attention to."

Rebecca Kempe

THE "BEAUTY"
OF MY EXISTENCE

I

When I was in eleventh grade, I wrote a throwaway prose poem called "Beauty" that haunted me for the rest of my high school career. It was half a page long, contained clichéd lines such as "I've hated myself" or "I've cursed my heritage for the way I look," and complained about my inability to fit traditional beauty standards. It was more of a rant than anything, wasn't meant to be polished, and I'd written it almost purely for the sake of performing at a Literary Arts coffeehouse.

For Literary Arts students, coffeehouses were part slam night, part formal reading, part theatrical chaos, and part whatever else we wanted them to be. They were held four nights a year, each hosted by a different grade, and we were all strongly encouraged to perform. There were almost no rules. You could perform anything as long as it was your work, wasn't too graphic or offensive, and required no special equipment. Most students stuck to reading more traditional forms of poetry or prose, but others performed songs, or stand-up comedy, or got friends to help them with table readings on stage. The audience size usually hovered between seventy and one hundred people: friends, classmates, teachers, and parents, all packed into the open space of our school library, the performers standing on a black riser stolen from the drama department, a single microphone on a stand. It was by far the least popular event run by any arts department at my school, but it was also the coziest and most intimate event, and the vibes and energy were always on point.

Coffeehouses were my safe space. I performed at almost every single one of them, experimenting with poetry and satire and stories and comedy, and I made a point of trying out new work on stage. I look back on these years as my "fearlessly vulnerable" era, when I thought nothing of writing so freely about my life, my failings, my relationships, and my family, then looking at a crowd and having to own those words. I performed poetry about my love for my siblings, about how much I worried for their sake despite not being close with them. I wrote some kind of rant about my hatred for the gifted program, and I wrote another one about learning to bike in my parents' basement. In a lot of ways, writing pieces for coffeehouses was what got me to take writing about my life more seriously, because it was where I first found evidence that an audience might care.

II

"Beauty" wasn't all that different in tone or degree of openness from anything I'd performed at previous coffeehouses. The poem was raw, but so was a lot of my earlier work; it was about my self-esteem issues, but I'd written about insecurity before; it contained some negative feelings about some of my family members, but I'd been less than flattering towards my parents before. But for some reason, the reception was a lot more positive than usual. It was standard to compliment people whose pieces you liked during intermission or at the end of the night, and I'd become used to hearing from a few people at each coffeehouse. But the vibe felt different. A lot more people came up to me than usual. A few others stopped me in the hallway to talk to me about it a few days later. I got the sense that people were obsessed with this poem.

I'd never written about being Black before, or at least, nothing I'd ever shown to anyone. This poem wasn't just about not feeling pretty; it was about feeling uglier than my mother, because her features looked more European than mine, about fitting the beauty standards for neither Black nor white women. I wasn't tall or curvy or toned or skinny and my hair was neither long nor straight. I was short, and my hair was short, nappy, and worn in cornrows. My feelings of physical unattractiveness were directly tied to my race. I couldn't write about my appearance without writing about my hair, or my facial structure, or my body shape, or my nose, and that inherently meant writing about being Black.

In hindsight, that's probably why people found the poem so memorable. The general demographic of my high school was white kids who wanted to be political. To me, nothing I was saying was groundbreaking. I'd grown up hearing stories of women who'd lost their jobs for daring to keep their hair natural, and I knew my hair was a statement of resistance. The current beauty standards valued looking white for anyone who wasn't white at birth, but I'd watched as white influencers used makeup and surgeries to look closer to mixed because they wanted to look "exotic." It felt a lot more like I was complaining; if my audience had been Black women, I'd have been preaching to the choir. But it wasn't, and I can only assume that it was a novel experience for the people in the audience to hear someone get up on stage and say these things. I guess from their perspective, I was being more vulnerable than usual, while from my perspective, I was just stating facts I'd known forever.

III

Against my better judgment, I allowed myself to be convinced to perform "Beauty" four more times, to much-less-curated audiences, in my high school's seven-hundred-seat auditorium. The first time around, I'd read it from a folded-up piece of paper I'd put into my back pocket before coffeehouse, but now, it had to be memorized, and I had to show up to rehearsals and dress up for the show. The stakes were higher now. I'd moved up to the big leagues.

The first two times I was asked to perform the poem, it was to represent the Literary Arts program at a showcase for potential incoming students. Eighth grade classes from various schools had been invited to attend, and while in the past, only the music and dance departments had performed at the showcases, this year, the arts coordinator wanted representatives from every department. My teacher wanted something short; he was a fan of the piece, and he thought it was great that I would be representing the program with a piece that had "a positive message." Honestly, I didn't think much of it at the time. I went to the rehearsals, performed in the two shows, and was sick of the poem by the end.

A few weeks later, I was dragged into performing the poem again, by one of my friends, who had remembered it from coffee-house a year earlier. Despite not being Black, she was one of the (mostly white) organizers for the school's first-ever Black History Month assembly. She'd pitched me as a performer to the other organizers without my consent, having decided I would be a great fit if only I would perform that poem again, and cornered me in the hallway to tell me about it approximately fifteen minutes before the first rehearsal. The team was disorganized. They hadn't secured enough speakers or performers and barely had a plan in mind. The teacher supervisor (also white) was very hands-off and nowhere to be seen. The organizer who had spearheaded the assembly, one of the few who was actually Black, had left due to major disagreements with the rest of the team. He'd left chaos in his wake, and none of the others understood how to run an event. Timelines were fuzzy—no one knew how long the rehearsal would take or when the next rehearsal would be or in what order the performances would happen. The tech crew volunteers were visibly unimpressed, and so was I. By some miracle the assembly wasn't a disaster.

I went along with it, because they were desperate, and because the person who'd dragged me in was my friend at the time. But I wish I hadn't, because by the end of that ordeal each and every student at the school knew my face.

This is the problem with being Black and being an artist: whenever you exist in mainstream places, it can never just be about your art. Because you're Black, and you're performing or creating in a predominately white space, you now have to repre-sent and take up space on the behalf of the Black community as a whole. Half the time, the curators will be non-Black people who have picked you specifically to perform Blackness to their audience, and Black aspiring curators will get pushed out. But not every Black person wants to make art about being Black all the time. Not everyone wants to be known mainly for talking about their race. I didn't sign up to be an activist. I don't really know what being Black even means. I barely have any culture or identity to draw from. I'm entirely the wrong person to be a representative.

IV

When I was in twelfth grade, my parents told me I'm lucky I have a last name that "doesn't sound Black." It's something I've been thinking about as I write this essay: whether or not I'm lucky that someone who comes across my work in print won't see me as Black unless it's mentioned or they see me in a photo, whether or not it's a kind of privilege, and whether or not I should use it.

I always feel uncomfortable writing about being Black, partly because I feel like my identity is more than just my race, but partly because I feel like people expect a narrative I simply can't provide. Growing up, I never had any friends who were Black or much contact with Black families other than my own. I always feel like people expect me to write about racist encounters (I've had some, but they were either minor or not things I want to dwell on), or about living in the hood or in poverty (I grew up in the suburbs), or about my culture (we didn't grow up with much African culture, and I'm not culturally Black in the North American way: classic diaspora problems), or about being an immigrant (except I grew up here, so I really don't feel like an immigrant), and so on. My skin is too dark to pass in the real world, but sometimes I wonder if I should just try passing in the "literary world": write what I feel like writing, make no allusions to my race in my bios while on submission, and let the editors glean whatever ethnicity clues they can from my name.

I've heard many authors speak about how in the publishing world, it's incredibly hard to publish as a writer of colour, and even harder if your books aren't about being a person of colour. It's part of the dual struggle we live with; we want to see ourselves represented in more stories, we want to be more represented in groups of people who publish stories, but we bear most of the responsibility for creating all of the representation. Most publishers would rather market books where we talk about being racialized people rather than books where we talk about existing as people who happen to be racialized. When we choose not to write about race at all, they tend to prioritize giving regular book slots to white authors, as if the realm of general human experience belongs mostly to people who aren't marginalized.

When my parents made their offhand comment about having a last name that passes as white, they were mostly referring to applying for jobs, because there's a smaller chance of my résumé being thrown out because a racist thinks it looks "too ethnic." But I also wonder if the same is true in literary spaces: if publishers will take longer to throw out my work if I never mention anywhere that I'm Black.

It feels wrong to say that I don't want to write stories about being a Black woman, because that's never been the entire truth. There is a reason why I wrote "Beauty." Being Black is part of my identity, and I can't always write about my life or worldview without it coming into play. But the more I interact with the artistic community, the more I feel like anyone with a visible identity gets sorted into a box, only getting taken out and displayed when it's convenient for other people. Being boxed in is tiring, and accidentally entering the box before being trapped into it is even more annoying.

It's not that I want to hide from any part of my identity. It's that I don't want to have to worry about not feeling "Black enough" or hitting some unsaid quota of racial commentary or political content. I don't want to write the type of story that ends up in lectures about social justice. I am Black and a woman, but I am not a Black woman first. All I want is the freedom to write whatever comes to mind. I just want to exist.

Sadiqa de Meijer

FOUND

I lost my notebook.

This was, for a few days that summer, my distracted answer when people asked me how I was.

It clearly wasn't a disaster, I wanted to convince myself, but my body seemed to argue; there was a void in my chest, and I couldn't relax, repeating my searches until they were senseless compulsions.

Only some of that discomfort had to do with the possibility of exposure—with someone, anyone, reading my private scribblings. Sure, it was unsettling to imagine eye contact with that individual, to be so inwardly naked, but after those seconds of awkwardness, I would have my notebook back; the universe would resume its semblance of order.

*

First, it was not in the three likeliest places. Not in my pocket, or in the maroon messenger bag, or on my desk. Then it wasn't in other bags either, or on the table, or in the corner of the living room where books tended to cluster. Not on the shelf by the phone, or the kitchen counter, or my dresser.

I searched every notebook-sized vacancy in our home: between the couch and its cushions, between furniture and walls, inside the furnace vents, among the toys.

Interrogating the four-year-old, trying to sound unalarming. *Did you play with it? Did you hide it?*

It wasn't in the alley between my locked bike and the door. Not on the sidewalks or in the gutters along recent routes of travel. And not in the sand of the playground, or in the grassy parking lot of the farm where I last wrote in it, or in the lost-and-found of the art gallery where I thought I had felt its weight in my pocket.

As I searched the neighbourhood, I found other things: a broken phone, a working MP3 player (mostly Beatles songs), a single children's shoe, a credit card, a ring, scraps of shopping lists (grapefruit, razors), and study notes (pulmonary physiology). I put up posters with the notebook's likeness. MISSING, REWARD. As I fastened them to buildings and lamp posts, neighbours and strangers commiserated. They told me of other, worse writerly losses: a car that was stolen with a hand-written poetry manuscript on the passenger seat, a novel on a computer in a room that flooded. Someone wrote *I hope and pray that you find it* on the poster in the grocery store.

It was a very rainy few days. If the notebook was outside, it was probably soaked. Maybe the ink of my name and phone number had blotted illegibly. Maybe it had been under the wheels of cars and trucks. Or maybe it was inside the house, and remained jammed in an unlikely corner, steps from where I slept.

*

And what was in it?

Things I thought, or saw, or overheard—whatever seemed to somehow matter, even though I couldn't yet say why. Almost a year's worth of writing, from minute cursive paragraphs to large, hurried scrawls.

There were notes from readings and other events—the idea of a reader feeling comfortable rather than spellbound within a work, a series of viewer responses to a friend's paintings.

A sight I walked past with my daughter one day: a man in a hard hat emerged from a house and started vomiting on the front lawn, and between each heave took one long drag from his cigarette.

Something I overheard while at that farm I mentioned: a jolly, elderly woman saying, *I'm covered in bug juice, the good stuff with lots of* DEET*!* I liked the words bug juice. I thought it was odd to praise DEET and organic strawberries in almost the same breath.

Serial attempts at describing the sound of pigeons cooing. Names of movies to see and books to read. How I felt in the hour before reuniting with a favourite teacher after almost two decades. The woman walking with a large, ornate wooden crucifix on her shoulder who paused and winked at me.

The unliterary, too: a recipe for yogurt, shopping lists, private intentions and admonitions, phone numbers, tasks.

And small drawings done for or by my daughter, from moments of amusing her, or instances when granting her my notebook gave me a few minutes of quiet. The progression in her forms over that year; from waving lines to rudimentary faces. My records of short conversations with her, the peculiar or endearing or funny statements that I wanted to remember.

I was doing the work of looking after her, along with part-time jobs that paid. I wasn't sleeping enough, or reading enough, and often it felt impossible to have an uninterrupted thought. I don't mean to overstate the difficulty; I could have written, I suppose, or someone in my circumstances could have written—but I didn't. Those years held bright and profound experiences, and they also made me feel that I might prove to be a writer only in my mind. My notebook, then, was the small but reliable dwelling where my potential self could live.

*

When I was a teenager, my mother found a poster on the curb on garbage day.

An image mounted on foam board. It's as tall as my waist, but before I went upstairs to take its measure, I wrote that it reaches my collarbones; it still feels larger than itself to me.

The poster advertises a long gone exhibition at the Rijksmuseum in Amsterdam, titled *Millet & Van Gogh*. The text and background are an electric red and blue, and leave a vivid retinal imprint. Below them are the deep vista and muted tones of Millet's well-known painting, *The Gleaners*.

When my mother gave me the poster, it was perfect, for reasons that seem submerged below the waters of what was actually happening.

We had been in Canada for a certain period. Not long enough for either of my parents to have secure employment, but long enough to feel a diminishing of the relationships with everyone we had left behind. A phase of shifting our weight, leaning more heavily on the new map.

I was close to leaving home. I wanted to study art, and my father was violently against it, and we fought until I gave in.

I was born in the neighbourhood south of the Rijksmuseum, on a short street named for Millet. It was where my mother had walked with me each day, in a blue stroller with a canvas top, naming what she saw.

The poster, when she found it, was like a beacon that lay both far behind and out in front of me.

*

The women in the painting glean; they gather what the harvesters have missed. One has lifted the bottom of her apron and tied its corners at her back to make a pocket. Each woman holds a small bundle of grain, which won't be enough to sell, but is for their private use.

In Agnes Varda's film, *The Gleaners and I*, the director follows contemporary French gleaners, who still pick the potatoes and grapes and apples left after the harvests. She also films urban gleaners, gathering food and other items from dumpsters or on the grounds of farmer's markets. Near the film's end, Varda acknowledges the metaphoric gleaning that she does with her camera, picking images from the field of visual possibilities.

Watching the documentary late that summer, I understood that my notebook was also a gleanings container. And later, in the wake of the film, another likeness arose in me. Leaving home, when home is a place that hurts, leads to the slow and strange revelation that the outside world is friendlier than the family that made you. It took me a long time, through many rooms and apartments, to trust that most days of my life would pass without anyone shouting at or threatening me; and then to know that I could leave relationships that repeated this ugliness. And the poster came with me, with its striking design.

I was gleaning not only as an aspiring writer, but also as a mother. Every day, feeling my own childhood pass through me almost too viscerally, I had to find what was worth saving from the rubble, what could be of use. To glean from farms is a matter of survival, but there is an urgency also in the impulse to glean from life; the animate scraps that might belong on a page, or become imprinted in a child's sense of self. And the harvester is time, a sickle or a combine, relentlessly clearing the ground.

*

I started a new notebook. My notes on Varda's film are in it. Tasks from a meeting of the parent committee at school. A short list of plants that grow in the trampled parts of the park: plantain, dandelion, clover.

A friend's phrase: *I'm moonlighting as a trauma surgeon.*

A list of subversive answers—meant to be closer at hand in conversation—to the question: where are you from?

Email addresses and phone numbers, some without any context that I can recall.

The words CLOSE THIRD PERSON! taking up a whole page.

A stern note to read Darwin.

The dimensions of our front window.

Lists of slant rhymes: panic/tonic, detector/doctored, elder/alder.

Occasionally, I remember something I've written down—the vague sense of a thought or idea with promise in it—and flip through the pages, and then realize that this material is in the old, lost notebook. There's a small ache then, and a flaring of *maybe*, maybe it will still return to me.

My daughter is at the stage now of pretending to write. I look at the pages with her attempts at script, consisting of string after string of loops, like a stretched old-fashioned telephone cord. She concentrates, her brow furrowed, and then she beams over the results. So the first writing is recursive; momentarily, it tricks the endless forward line and circles back. Hovers protectively over the present, then makes a loop that can hold it.

Tom Rachman

CONFESSIONS OF
A LITERARY SCHLUB

As my flight descended over the turquoise Caribbean, I asked myself, Who'd go to the Cayman Islands and attend a literary event of mine? I soon learned the answer: nobody. Just empty chairs and an awkward bookseller. "Maybe you could swim with stingrays tomorrow?" she suggested. "They always turn up."

Promoting a book can derange you. After years of quiet toil and noisy typing, you clutch a published book, and step forth to meet the public, eight billion humans who, mystifyingly, seem not to know that your new novel just came out.

Occasionally, someone treats you like the important writer you long to be (but probably aren't). They rave about your prose and frown attentively when you speak. It's an adrenaline shot to your ego. Then, you're at a signing table, the pile of hardcovers all unsold, and everyone has gone. You're just another needy nobody, your ego mashed underfoot.

Now and then, a literary novelist is swept to fame. But most are swept by the polar wind of indifference. To avert oblivion, authors today attempt to twist themselves into hucksters, the spokesmodels for their books, sales rep of their inner lives.

I'd like to blame tech. I try to blame it for everything.

When the internet bulldozed the traditional press, it squashed book coverage too. But the internet flung up alternatives, from literary websites to BookTok to public readings on Zoom.

Finally, novelists didn't need the gatekeepers. They could shout for attention themselves. On the downside, they had to shout for attention themselves.

Publishers and agents—rarely certain why one decent book soars when a thousand more go plop—pressured authors to become more accessible, not merely slouching around festivals and bookshops, but thrusting themselves forward for inspection on Goodreads and Twitter and making themselves reachable via direct message. The writerly myth altered.

Previously, biographies and gossip imagined The Novelist as a tormented character, pungent from debauchery, infidelity, booze. Now, the writers who prevailed seemed assertively nice: the endearing quirks, the correct politics.

Being beastly never made anyone talented at writing. Nor does being kind to cats. My point is: the skill set for literature is not necessarily the skill set for promoting it.

Imagine Dostoevsky, nagged to update his Facebook page. Or Emily Dickinson at a poetry slam, posting on Instagram. Or Kafka addressing his fans on YouTube: "Hey, guys! Brutal wakeup today: I open my eyes, and I'm, like, an insect—what is up with that?! Check out my new story, #Metamorphosis. Hit 'like,' and subscribe below!"

Consider the case of Suzanne Young, author of a young-adult horror novel, who turned up for her reading in Phoenix, and found that she outnumbered the audience. Young tweeted a photo of the deserted store, with the caption, "If you ever want to see a career low point, this is it. Crying my entire way home."

She didn't sob for long. Her tweet went viral, and she ended up on NBC Nightly News, living a plot twist worthy of feel-good fiction: because nobody turned up, she had a hit.

What is the moral of her story? That the internet can save us? Or that bookstore readings are a waste, and you're better off hyping yourself online?

For today's author, the trail of shamelessness begins before the novel is published—perhaps before it's written. Developing an online fanbase inhibits your writing, but your career may depend upon it. (Before her sorrowful event, Young already had more than twelve thousand Twitter followers, who helped circulate her post, ultimately seen by 7.9 million people.)

Once you've produced a manuscript, your self-abasement picks up, as you beg blurbs from any noted writer you've chanced to meet and failed to alienate. This means published ex-classmates from the creative writing MFA; or prominent authors who taught you there; or the bestselling novelist you importuned at a literary festival.

Superficially, the blurb is a recommendation to readers. But it's also a flex, showing that a novel's author is connected, high-status, has cool friends.

Every blurb request is inappropriate. You're demanding twenty hours or more from a busy professional, all to serve your interests, and with questionable impact. Moreover, you're asking an author to mislead their readers, given that most blurbs are plainly dishonest: there simply isn't that much genuine gushing.

Next, you must badger your followers and family to preorder your novel, as advanced sales cue the publisher to take it seriously and promote yours rather than the flood of other books released at the same time. To attract coverage, you need a narrative behind the narrative—that your fiction is actually non-fiction in disguise, inspired by your messy divorce, your messy kids, your drug bust, your life in the burbs, your PTSD, your OCD, your impotence, your incontinence, your pet marmot Ernesto.

What you mustn't say is that you just made up the story, that it came purely from imagination. Fellini, I once heard, falsified personal anecdotes to publicize his movies. I've been tempted to try this, to spin yarns and present myself as charismatic. But I can't bring myself to lie. I remain a schlub making cups of tea in my kitchen.

You also must write for free. Now that the media has fragmented into many outlets of varied intent, you cannot hope that a mighty publication will crown your book. Even the cover of the *New York Times Book Review* has far less effect than it had. Once, it meant instant bestseller. Today, with everyone reading on phones, there is no "cover" in the same way.

So, you churn out self-publicizing content in disguise, everywhere from upstart literary blogs to old-media websites—free contributions like "The 7 Best Books on the Subject I Just Wrote About." This bewilders me, that you're supposed to promote your book by exhorting people to buy other books. You must pray they'll notice your mini-bio and click the Amazon link.

Needless to say, you schlep to any event that'll have you. The organizers are delightful; they revive your faith in contemporary literature and restore your longing for a place in it. Then, you're looking out from a lectern at seven people, three of whom are personal friends. You wonder if any of this makes sense.

Book events expose a fundamental flaw in promoting fiction: novelists tend to be mumblers with bad haircuts who can't bring their writing to life before a crowd and are inarticulate when answering questions about the craft. Some are performers; some are insightful; some, inspiring. More are the dinner guest nobody notices, but who has thoughts, and gathers them, composes them, types them in private, revises and revises—and only then, finds the words.

One of my first bookstore readings was at Politics & Prose in Washington, DC. Beforehand, the organizers stashed me in a sideroom alongside a staffer on break, whose calm contrasted with my terror. In minutes, I'd need to declaim about literature. I had no right. I was an imposter.

After the event, my sister rushed over, assuring me I hadn't humiliated myself. "You didn't seem nervous at all," she said.

"Tranquilizers," I confided. "I took many tranquilizers."

According to a recent survey conducted by the *Bookseller* magazine, the majority of debut authors say book publication damaged their mental health. At least one respondent ended up on meds.

But writing careers have always been marked more by failure than glory. And blurbs, public readings, mass indifference—all that preceded the internet era.

Is any of this truly new?

When it comes to contemporary literature, you hear debates about identity and appropriation, about awards and autofiction. But what matters is the competition: those words and pictures and videos heating the device in your pocket, which vibrates so impatiently, goading you to check its stories.

While the internet is the most powerful marketing tool that writers have ever had, the internet is also devastating to an art that requires close concentration.

Once, brainy types read contemporary novels for amusement, to ponder what it meant to be human, to shock themselves at what others did privately, to join the intelligentsia, to march into the debate. This role is rarely taken by a novel today.

A subculture of ultraliterary types does still rally around the latest darlings of fiction. A bigger constituency buys the novels selected for TV book clubs or by prize juries. Most years, a screen-adapted literary work joins the bestseller list. But beneath those few titles are stacks and stacks of disappointment.

The study of literature dwindles too, as with the rest of the humanities. According to a report in *The Times* of London, one university had two hundred English-literature undergrads a decade ago; now, it's down to thirty.

When I meet bookish types with young-adult offspring, many speak of how their kids devoured fiction when little, but have since abandoned it. What those middle-aged bookish types are ashamed to add is that they themselves—with extensive culture and extensive bookshelves—scarcely read fiction anymore.

One culture critic told me that he still reviews novels because that way he is forced to read them. Authors have made similar admissions to me.

Will Lloyd, a journalist at the political and literary magazine the *New Statesman*, noticed that he'd read plenty of books lately—and none was a novel. So, he spent a week quizzing the literary types he knew, asking whether they were reading fiction, if they discussed it with friends, if they sought it out for social insights. Among forty people, only two said yes.

I feared that I was an imposter in writing. I've come to wonder if all literary novelists are imposters now, barging into the far edge of the culture, holding up reams of pages, saying, I wrote something—look at it!

How presumptuous: engaging in make-believe, asking strangers to admire it. Those strangers too have something to say, and nowadays can, commenting, filming, liking, downvoting.

What's odd about being a novelist today is that the position retains a shimmer of prestige with only a glimmer of audience.

Or maybe I'm wrong. Maybe it's just *my* writing that is shrivelling away. Maybe I'm projecting my eclipse onto the field.

I wouldn't fight that charge. I'm tired of fighting for attention, imploring strangers to care about what I cared about, pleading for a hearing of my voice in an art that seems quieter and quieter, that is missing the point somehow.

A New York book editor told me that publishing had always been this way: a few megahits support all those below. Even writers at the top are rarely satisfied. Philip Roth, who had success after success, died bitter that he hadn't won the Nobel Prize, the editor remarked, wondering just how much would be enough to quench authors.

A few weeks ago, I visited a smattering of London bookshops at the request of my British publisher. Sheepishly, I approached staff, mentioning that I was supposed to sign my new novel. They hunted down a few copies. I always feel absurd autographing books.

But it's thrilling too, if you don't look down: that someone was crazy enough years ago to fly me to the Cayman Islands for a reading.

I've been an imposter, unsure what I was doing here, frazzled by a caterwauling, distracted, outraged world, my thoughts firing, hesitating to say them—so I put them onto paper, fighting with sentences, removing commas only to replace them, judging myself a failure, hating that I minded, despairing at my irrelevance, writing to cure myself, wanting to say something that'd make others listen, trying, trying, mostly failing.

A writer.

Jessica Moore

//////////////

SHADOW FACE

Sometimes my life opens its eyes in the dark.
—Tomas Tranströmer, translated
from the Swedish by Patricia Crane

1. All through the winter, spring, and summer of my twins' first year, I think about what it means to be so porous as a mother. The state of care and openness I sometimes feel, letting my edges go, sensing beyond myself, can be a sort of bliss. I hold baby S. or baby A. and close my eyes, lean my mind toward the invisible of them. Their essence. I sit in the backyard and breathe in the bergamot, let a channel open to the heavy, slow bees. Merging can be full of pleasure.

2. The character of Lila in Elena Ferrante's Neapolitan Novels, translated into English by Ann Goldstein, describes a different kind of porousness. *Smarginatura*, which suggests bleeding outside the frame, is a printer's technical term that literally means to cut off the margins of a page. Ferrante uses it to gesture to something psychic, multiple; Goldstein translates this as "dissolving

margins." Lila first experiences this "malaise," "a feeling of disin-tegration of mental and bodily boundaries," on New Year's Eve, standing on a crowded terrace in Naples as fireworks begin to explode. "She had the impression that something absolutely material, which had been present around her and around every-one and everything forever, but imperceptible, was breaking down the outlines of persons and things and revealing itself." This other kind of porousness—a fragmenting, a rupture, in which she is threatened by "something absolutely material" hovering just below the surface—leaves her unhinged, terrorized.

3. In the second COVID-19 winter, I become swallowed by a sus-penseful television series called *Behind Her Eyes*, which is, in part, about people who practise astral travel. Souls glide from room to room as shimmering lights and can even occupy another person's body if their soul, too, is out wandering. I watch at arm's length, drawn like a fluttering thing and simultaneously repelled. I can't look away. Something familiar stirs.

4. For years, I've carried in the back of my mind a scene I read (Was it Bachelard? Was it Proust?) of a living room gone strange. In it, the narrator, a child, comes down the stairs to find the familiar room transformed. Same chairs in the same positions, same clock ticking on the mantel. Nothing out of place, but the sense that everything is different. It haunts me. I push to recall where I first read it—I recognize that feeling. And I love the sim-plicity with which this writer (Who?) describes it. Green. Empty. The room exactly the same, yet undeniably other.

One of the swells in my book *The Whole Singing Ocean* leads to the lines "nothing so horrifying as something different / in the shape of someone you know." When I wrote this, I was thinking about night terrors and transgression, and looking back, I can see: the prickling sense I knew intimately, the one that led me to write those words, is the fissure that let the green living room in.

5. This prickling sense fits the definition of Freud's uncanny (*unheimlich*)—"that class of terrifying that leads us back to something long known to us, once very familiar." I come across this quote while reading Erin Wunker on mothers and their strangeness, their unknowable core, her own mother disappearing in the wee hours each morning into deep black water and swimming alone across the lake. In the original German, *unheimlich* opposes *heimlich*—literally "homey." (Something interesting happens here with the prefix *un*—as Sherry Simon points out in her reading of Anne Carson's *Economy of the Unlost*, "negation has the added advantage of economy." The word *unheimlich* works double time, containing and conveying both the root word (*heimlich*) and its opposite. In Carson's own words: "Two realities for the price of one.") There is a loss in English of the direct parallel—*uncanny/canny* does not capture it—between something eerie and that which is cozy, friendly, familiar.

But *heimlich* also means *secret*, or *hidden*—the way the person we know best can hide so many faces.

Something different in the shape of someone you know.

6. At a traffic light on the way to preschool one morning, I tip the rear-view mirror down to see the twins in the back seat, both solemn (rainy day, scuffle getting out the door). Both cried about one thing or another, about my sharpness in the rush. I turn now to smile at A., and she says,

—Mama, sometimes when Mama smiles I feel sad. And some-times when Mama feels sad, I smile.

It jolts me, this expression of the ways we are impacted by each other. I turn back to the road, catch her eye in the mirror.

—Are you sad now? I ask.

—No. Hey, I can see Mama's eyes! Her gaze flicks between me and the mirror, and then she says,

—When Mama does that, Mama's shadow face turns the other way! She corrects herself. Mama's *reflection.*

But I'm haunted by this term, *shadow face,* and by the hidden mysteries of the people closest. What might they see in me that I don't even know is there?

7. When I was a child, someone—my mother, I suppose—explained that alcohol alters people. She must have said this because I noticed people acting louder or alien at a party at our house, and the way I understood it was that drinking made you *a different person,* as though, yes, a spirit were a thing in a bottle you could drink down or pour out. I remember scrutinizing my mother's flushed and laughing face when she put me to bed at that party, waiting for the unfamiliar being to betray itself in some unsettling gesture or flicker of the eyes. Watching for that other person I knew she had become, light from the kitchen leaning in.

8. At the aquarium, in the relentlessness of March-break crowds, the blue dark and the rush of voices, the corridors down which S. keeps nearly disappearing, corridors down which A. clings staunchly to my hand, I miss nearly everything, attention shat-tered. I finally lure S. in close with a snack, and when I turn to the nearest exhibit, I see the sea dragon. Feathery and slight,

violet and brown. Fluted fins on its back sway in unseen currents; its whole body sways, drifting in ribbons of seaweed near the aquarium floor. How soothed I feel, watching. For brief seconds, with both children pressed against my legs, I tune out the harried, half-dark world and lean my forehead against the glass. The sea dragon, the plaque tells me, uses mainly passive locomotion, mostly *is moved by* currents around it.

9. There are times when, in the fray of S. and A., in the stream of them, both talking while they clamber over me, pulling in different directions, saying *Mama, Mama*, louder and louder, I wonder who (and if?) I am. If I exist beyond the desires of my children. Is the sea dragon without desire? Is such submission to be aspired to? Or is the comfort I felt with my head pressed to the glass only the false comfort of surrendering what's true, what's mine? (The wedge-shaped core of darkness within, as described by Virginia Woolf's matriarch in *To the Lighthouse*: my deep treasure.) In the same way my organs were shouldered aside during pregnancy—dislocated, rearranged—so do I feel in this constant current of my two small people. I have to fight to hold onto my own will, my own self.

Fragmented. Sidelined. And is there fear here? Is there, perhaps, a long-toothed thing lurking nearby? A devouring thing—dark, eating, edgeless.

10. "Ah, . . . to no longer hear the demands of their flesh as commands more pressing, more powerful than those which came from mine," writes Goldstein in her translation of Ferrante's *The Lost Daughter*.

11. Long before the twins, I went to Golden Lake with a beautiful, golden man. We had met on a farm in the heat of July, kneeling among the brassicas. We inched closer as the harvesting days went on. Grew sharp as blades in our desire, walked an edge of my making: I set limits, I'm not totally sure I could explain why, except it was a time in my life when I was trying in concrete ways to keep certain parts of myself to myself.

The golden man knew a herbalist near Golden Lake. When we arrived that afternoon, rumpled, hot, I was unsure of the dog and the dog was unsure of me, nosing my hand and skittering back, deep black and watchful. The herbalist led us to the barn where we would sleep. Leaves of sweet gale, laid out to dry, covered the floor of the loft. Sweet gale is said to help with lucid dreaming. Before we went to sleep that night, under the mosquito net, we blurred our edges, made a pact to try to meet in dreams.

12. One of the characters in the television series with travelling souls is the child of a single mother. He doesn't know what she's up to, learning to leave her body. He's only eight. Sometimes while I'm watching, my legs twitch as though the ground beneath me is not to be trusted. Nothing is sure. The series builds to a bottoming-out reveal: the person we understood to be the main character throughout was, in fact, someone else. And now, although the single mother's body, face, and eyes are still here, she herself is gone. Her child is in the care of something different.

13. The knife made me porous in a perilous way, and they pumped poisons into my veins to protect me. I was made dangerously permeable so my babies could be born.

Just before I went into the room with the knife, when they'd tried and failed three times to place the epidural, I experienced a moment beyond myself. I was offered a gas to breathe, and I took it. I inhaled and rose up, up, feeling something eagle-like lifting me, something strong and airborne, and it wasn't that I couldn't feel the long needle piercing that most tender column of nerves, it wasn't that I didn't know pain—it was only that, up there, I didn't care. I was winged, I was elsewhere.

14. The golden man and I kissed and kissed, turning liquid. Another kind of dissolving, another counterpoint to smargina-tura, molten and willed. His fingers left long bruises on my thighs. We came to the edge. After, when he was asleep, I lay listening to the outside singing, the wild orchestra of summer. I wandered in that state between waking and sleeping until I crossed over and then, sometime later, surfaced sharply—into the blackest of black. I couldn't even see the mosquito net. I'd been having the clearest sensation—ebullient!—of being cradled in the vast dear space between stars and then, all at once, flipped upside down. It was so surprising I let out a sound—*ha!*

15.—Is Mama ever scared Mama will turn into a green dragon?

A. and I are walking hand in hand back from the lake. My eyes grow wide.

—No, I say.

I'm scared all the time that I will disintegrate, become lost in the streaming debris of all that's asked of me, every day, but I have not been afraid that something else—something monstrous—will appear in my place.

—Are you sometimes scared of that? I ask, and she says,

—Yes.

—When are you scared of that?

—When Mama's eyes are green.

My eyes are always green.

16. For Lila, there is a way in which we as human beings are "insufficient," and the entity that waits beneath the surface is the most real of all. "It was—she told me—as if, on the night of a full moon over the sea, the intense black mass of a storm advanced across the sky, swallowing every light." Here is the image that has remained with me: a shadowed shape moving closer from a far horizon. In my mind, there is a woman alone watching it, and she is standing at the edge of her desire.

17. We stave off TV for as long as we can, but when the twins are three and we are desperate to sleep in, at least some of the time, we download a season of the original *Scooby-Doo*. With bleary eyes, I set up the computer for them at 5:30 a.m., then stumble back to bed. The Mystery Gang of five cartoon characters solves a case each episode, laugh track *hahaha*ing in the background, and through the show's formulaic denouement, the phantom, ghoul, or monster is always revealed to be a minor character. Every time, one of the members of the gang reaches out a hand from offscreen and lifts the mask, and every time, the villain is someone they know.

—Can we watch a Scoob? whispers S. before first light.

They race to the couch and huddle together. A. sits still, attentive, hands held close to her body as the spooky tale begins, but S. is soon bouncing up and down, the sensations inside him too big to contain.

18. Waking into the blackest of black is like not really waking at all. It's like being in the depths of yourself, floating somewhere behind your eyes. That night in the barn, when I woke to the sound of my own voice, I used touch instead of sight. My hands found the edge of the net and the floor with its carpet of drying leaves. My feet nudged the leaves aside until they felt the trap door, where I lowered myself down the ladder. Like moving through water, ink. Outside the open barn door, my toes touched the grass, the lush silver-green feel of it. Shapes, barely there, of other buildings, trees. I crouched and peed, and from the dark came a shape, blacker than night, bearing down upon me. (Was this what Lila felt?)

A thin lick of fear spread up the centre of my chest but there was no time to react or evade the dark thing coming. The black dog traced a circle around me, sniffing the ground I had marked.

19. When I learned that entities could attach onto people during surgeries, coming in through that knife opening, I was afraid. I looked back over the two years since the twins were born and saw all the ways we were cursed. In those ragged hours, I wasn't seeing the countless gifts, the care, the meals and myriad arms. Instead, my night-mind whirred with wronging: the eviction, the hospital's indifference, the fights with friends, some of whom I lost for good. I was seeing the anger, new and swift, a fierce mass that loped through me without warning, blotting out the moon.

20. In a search for reflections on Woolf's portrayal of mother-hood in *To the Lighthouse*, I stumble across the piece that holds the un/familiar room. Anne Carson. Of course it is Anne Carson! In her essay, "Every Exit Is an Entrance," she describes her earli-est memory, which is of a dream she had when she was about

three years old. She comes down the stairs in her own house to find the living room looking exactly as it always had, "and yet it was utterly, certainly, different. Inside its usual appearance the living room was as changed as if it had gone mad."

What she describes is so known to me, so deep within, that either she is drawing upon something larger than herself, collective and spreading, or else I have absorbed the words and sensations of someone else into my own being. The green living room is alive in me too.

"There is in her [Carson's] work a persistent consciousness of intruding realities," writes Simon. "We are directed to the place where the shadow's edge joins the black of night, reminded always that surfaces have seams, an underlife."

21. In the morning, I told the golden man about the feeling of being flipped upside down, and the sense I'd had that there was a trick to it, that I had been on the verge of getting beyond myself.

I had a feeling he would have something to say, he who proclaimed to be a bodhisattva. (Are you allowed to call yourself that? I wondered. And here I thought he was just a boy from Burlington.) He told me astral travel usually involves a reversal: at the moment of exiting the body, people nearly always report a sensation of being turned upside down.

—You almost got there, he said, lifting my hair to clasp my neck and pull my mouth to his.

22. Lying between the twins at bedtime, I feel S.'s body begin to release into that other space, his eyelids already too heavy to keep open. But A. is awake with the story I just finished telling— an Irish changeling tale—and now fairies who would steal a

human baby and leave one of their own in its place are running through our minds. Parts of my childhood are woven of images from a song, the one made of a Yeats poem about a child spirited away, "Where the wandering water gushes / From the hills above Glen-Car / In pools among the rushes / That scarce could bathe a star," and I sing it now to my own two human children before they cross over into dreams.

—One day can we go to Glen-Car? asks A., her head resting on my shoulder, her hand holding my hand firmly against her belly, as though asking me to pin her here.

23. I'm always waiting for something completely unthought of to tumble out of me, for these words I've written to transmute and expand, become *other*—leaving a changeling child in their place. Greater than anything I could have conceived of. Greater than me.

24. The winter I was pregnant, I had somehow separated from myself, fragmented, as though I were standing somewhere behind my life. A new kind of darkness formed. Not *because* I was pregnant, but its threat made more urgent by the imminence of two people I already wanted to protect. Something in me was stuck, the wedge-shaped core webbed over, untended, and rather than a fortress or a retreat, I found myself in a state of over-porousness. I had no edges. I would drag myself from bed late in the mornings and walk to the boardwalk where I melted into that one cradling tree (branches like a hand strong enough to hold me) for the temporary relief of being nothing, cold waves against the breakwater, gulls screaming overhead.

How I wanted to rush rush rush to fix my sadness. How can you shield someone who's inside you from what's inside you?

25. And then, in the midst of all that darkness, a moment like a lamp—

26. In March of that edgeless winter, something came to wake me in the depths of night. Before I'd even opened my eyes, I felt it. In the centre of my chest. A warmth, a light.

I'd heard of the old hag who comes to sit on your chest in the night and suffocate you. I'd even felt her once, in a winter long before. But this, the hag's opposite, never. Joy radiating out from me and sending bright warm rays into the darkness before I remembered the grey. Joy like a hand shaking me, saying, Look, look! Wake up! There's this too.

27. In thinking of Lila's "dissolving margins," I'm reminded of Luce Irigaray and her writings on women and leakiness. I remember the relief, the giddiness I felt at nineteen, sitting on the steps outside the university lecture hall on a windswept day reading the words "deux lèvres qui se touchent" ("two lips caressing each other"—the labia) and her thoughts on fluidity and leaking—literally, in the form of breast milk, menstrual and amniotic fluid—after the long, dry, masculine desert of a first-year survey course of Western philosophy. Irigaray, it seemed to me, poked gleefully at the notion that women cannot be trusted because they are constantly spilling over, open to the world. Porous.

Are we, as mothers I mean, meant to have no boundaries?

28. When I go looking for what precisely Irigaray wrote about women and leakiness, I find an article with this sentence: "The feminine cannot be known as feminine (as sexuate difference) within a phallogocentric logic because this logic is predicated on

rigid and static forms, solid truth and *knowable entities*" (my emphasis). A shiver goes through me. Because, in addition to whatever shifting fluid truth was mine already, the alteration that comes with motherhood is unutterable.

29. Who is this new woman? What does she share with the one who came before? I know we're not meant to be finite or fixed. In Tomas Tranströmer's poem "Romanska bågar" (Romanesque arches), the vaults of a church offer an eloquent metaphor for the endless chambers contained within each human being. "Valv gapande bakom valv" ("Vault opening behind vault"—Robert Bly's translation or "Vault gaped behind vault"—Robin Fulton's): Tranströmer and his translators saw the massive, the manifold of us.

I myself wrote, "I am changed, I am multiple," after becoming a mother. There's something slippery to it, though, a slippage of surety, of something to hold on to.

30. I know A. was seeing something true when she said, "Mama's shadow face." And I believe Lila is right, and Sherry Simon in her reading of Anne Carson as well: there is an underlife, a shadow pressing behind every person and room, an other in the shape of whom and what we know.

"Now that we were mothers," writes Deborah Levy with almost quizzical incredulity,

> we were all shadows of our former selves, chased by the women we used to be before we had children. We didn't really know what to do with her, this fierce, independent young woman who followed us about, shouting and pointing the finger while we wheeled our buggies in the English

rain.... We did not have the language to explain that we were not women who had merely "acquired" some children—we had metamorphosed...into someone we did not entirely understand.

31. I hold both the shadow and the lamp. Who—or what—else might live inside me, now?

For a time I contained three hearts.

32. Sometimes my life opens its eyes in the dark.

Michelle Cyca

///////////

BIG BABIES

When my son was six weeks old and there was little to do but fill the blurry days pushing his stroller from one arbitrary destination to another, I took him shopping at my favourite consignment store. As I walked around, he woke up and let out a piercing wail. I was already pivoting his stroller toward the exit when an employee looked up at me. "Oh," she said knowingly, "that's a new-baby cry." She and another employee rushed to gaze at my furious, tiny baby while I prepared to apologize. "Mine never liked the stroller either," she said. "Would you like me to hold him while you shop?"

I've often been struck by the unexpected generosity of strangers toward my babies, perhaps because I've absorbed the rhetoric that a noisy child is a blight on society. Recently, in Vancouver, a furious debate erupted online after an application to expand a daycare in a residential neighbourhood was denied, partly on the grounds that nearby residents objected to the noise. "I can't escape the noise currently, so if she were to expand this daycare, we would have no peace," one person argued in a hearing, as reported by journalist Dan Fumano. His column in the *Vancouver Sun* ignited an online firestorm of opprobrium, much of it from dismayed parents chasing the pipe dream of securing a child care spot (Vancouver has only one space for every five three-to-five-year-olds). But there was an undercurrent of sympathy for the aggrieved neighbours. "Children don't just laugh," columnist Sandy Garossino asserted on social media, while radio host Buzz Bishop complained about living next door to a daycare: "It's eternal toddler preschool noise and it's very irritating."

It's true: children, especially babies, make noise. Many people would say kids are fine if they are quiet and unobtrusive—which is to say, if they don't behave at all like kids. Earlier this year, a Southwest Airlines passenger had a meltdown over a crying baby, captured in a TikTok video that went viral. Airplanes are designed to maximize discomfort and unwanted intimacy, and as such, they're a frequent locus of anti-baby sentiment. "You're yelling," a flight attendant cautions, and the man screams, "So is the baby! Did this motherfucker pay extra to yell?" On video, it's comedic; in person, it's every parent's worst nightmare: becoming the target of society's mounting intolerance toward children. Even when they're happy, babies are often unwelcome. On Reddit's "Am I the Asshole?" forum—a crowdsourced gauge of social mores—one user recently asked whether making their infant laugh in a restaurant was rude, particularly since another diner asked them to stop. The prevailing sentiment was yes. "There's nothing wrong with your kid laughing, but there's a time and a place for it," one poster replied.

What is the time and place for children? Often, the pro- and anti-child camps split along the question of whether or not kids are, fundamentally, annoying. Many people are quick to argue that the sounds of children are beautiful and life affirming.

While I appreciate people sticking up for crying babies, I also think it's the wrong question. The right one is whether children are members of society, or whether we should treat them less like people and more like dogs (to whom they are compared frequently).

In some cultures, the answer to this question is implicit. Indigenous spaces tend to be very baby friendly, and the idea of censuring a child for shrieking is unthinkable among my Indigenous friends and family. You see babies at every ceremony and event, which makes their presence unremarkable. They're part of the community, and everyone shares in the task of looking out for them. Many other cultures outside of North America have a similarly inclusive approach; when my husband and I visited Japan, we marvelled at groups of unescorted schoolchildren. The long-running Japanese show *Old Enough!*, which features children embarking on their first independent errands, captivated viewers when it hit Netflix in 2022 with its vision of a society where toddlers might venture out alone to the grocery store.

The prevailing North American attitude views letting your child out of your sight momentarily as negligence, while approaching a child you don't know is similarly taboo. In 2017, a single father in Vancouver was investigated by the Ministry of Family and Child Services for letting his children, who ranged in age from seven to eleven, take the bus to school alone after he had spent two years teaching them how to navigate transit. There are similar stories of American parents investigated and even arrested for letting their kids walk home alone from parks or playgrounds. These incidents underscore how conditional the participation of children in society is; even when they are quiet and orderly, some adults will remind them that they do not belong.

While the most vehement anti-child positions are the fringe views of a small but vocal minority, the rejected Vancouver day-care is an example of a real-world impact, one that compounds the challenges of parenting without social support. Parenting is already a hard and lonely gig, one that got harder and lonelier during the pandemic. But it's not just parents who are feeling isolated. In 2021, four in ten Canadians reported feeling lonely some or all of the time. The pandemic insulated us from regular human contact, and many have emerged with a heightened sensitivity to others. Everyone else seems louder, more annoying, more obtrusive. The *New York Times*, investigating the growing phenomenon of "consumer rage," pointed to the "frictionless economy" of online, depersonalized transactions as one cause: many of us have been sold on the idea that our daily lives should be populated with easy, efficient, painless interactions. And children, in all their irrepressible raucousness, are friction. The transactional nature of modern life has led many adults to believe that if they are paying for a restaurant meal, an airline seat, or a house in a nice neighbourhood, they should be entitled to dictate the terms of their experience—and to exclude those who disrupt it.

This is an impoverished and self-defeating perspective. We all begin our lives dependent on the tenderness of adults, and if we're very lucky, we'll grow old enough to rely on others' care again. At any point in between, we may become disabled or ill, or we may experience a mental health crisis, a serious injury, or just a really bad day. It's only temporary good fortune that prevents any of us from becoming the friction in someone else's existence. When we inevitably do, we should hope that others treat us with compassion. Enjoying a serene restaurant meal is nice, but it is in our collective self-interest to cultivate a more tolerant society.

At the consignment store, I thanked the shop employee for her offer to hold my baby and took him outside in the sun to soothe him. These moments of spontaneous kindness from strangers linger in my mind: a young man wordlessly lifting the front wheels of my stroller over a high curb; a fellow passenger whispering, "You deserve a glass of wine," after my baby cried through the last forty-five minutes of a flight; a grandfather at the playground kneeling to gently wiggle my daughter's shoe back onto her foot. To brush against one another's insufferable humanity and turn toward it with kindness rather than irritation is, to me, the substance of community. Sometimes that humanity is loud, but it's always beautiful.

Christine Lai

NOW MUST
SAY GOODBYE

The Embankment. *how do you like this one. we are nearly* London.

MONUMENTS

The scene is quiet, the Thames embankment nearly empty. In the bottom left-hand corner, a barely visible figure stands by the parapet. Farther along the embankment: the obelisk. Made of granite mined from the ancient quarries by the Nile, Cleopatra's Needle was first erected in Heliopolis and subsequently moved to Alexandria, where it was later toppled, buried, and, millennia later, excavated before being transported to the city. Here it still sits, on a plinth that holds a time capsule containing photographs, children's toys, coins, a map of London, hairpins, and newspapers.

NATURAL DISASTERS

In that vast city, I began collecting in a time of dispersal. At an ephemera fair, I came across a vintage postcard depicting Cologne Cathedral, which I was supposed to visit with someone who was no longer by my side. The image made me cry, but I purchased it anyway. Something about the cheapness and fragility of the diminutive picture spoke to my experience at the time. Perhaps love is the found object par excellence, the most transient and aleatory thing collected.

I became an habitué of ephemera fairs and flea markets. The poet Paul Éluard once wrote to his ex-wife about his habit of hoarding postcards in the aftermath of their divorce: "[I] stay in this apartment arranging my cards. In postcard style, I am crowned with melancholy, decline and neglect." I too stayed in to arrange my cards. The collecting and organizing structured my days, and the time of heartbreak receded.

Éluard understood this truth about the *cartes postales*: they not only provide fodder for meditations on the past, but also facilitate an alchemical process by which the flux of existence is transformed into order and calm.

To Miss Alice Taylor, Watford, Hertfordshire
January 9, 1905
Dear Alice,
Thanks for P/C last week; would have answered it before but I haven't been well and it "slipt my memory." Am now much better. Nance says she is quite aware you are alive, but as she wrote last it is your turn to write. Now must say goodbye. Best wishes to all + kind regards, Ted.

LOVERS

In the novel *Cartes Postales* (1973), by Frédéric Vitoux, the narrator discovers a trove of vintage postcards, and proceeds to trace the contours of imaginary lives using both the explicit content and the implicit meaning of the messages.

The postcard, for all its openness, resembles a small, enclosed room, wherein two individuals conduct an intimate conversation. Even in the plainest messages, it is possible to intuit an entire past, shared between sender and recipient, that underpins the correspondence. As Jennifer Croft writes, "It is apparently a paradox that the first essential qualities of postcards, brevity and exposure, are guarantors of closeness (despite separation), emblems of intimacy."

When Heinrich von Stephan, a German postal service official, proposed the idea of the *offenes Postblatt* (open post-sheet) in 1865, his goal was to expedite communication, to allow for "sufficient simplicity and brevity." After the first postcards began circulating in 1869 in Austria-Hungary, there were initially concerns about privacy. To evade the voyeur's eye, senders wrote encrypted messages in code and shorthand, in Latin or Esperanto;

some wrote upside down or backwards; others communicated romantic sentiments by positioning the stamp in a particular way. The limitation of space placed constraints upon language yet also liberated it, initiating new ways of writing.

BUSY PERSON'S CORRESPONDENCE CARD

HELLO		I SPEND MY TIME	
PAL	SUGAR	MOTORING	
FOLKS	HUBBY	HIKING	
CHUM	WIFEY	BOATING	
THIS PLACE IS		FISHING	
QUIET	NOISY	READING	
IDEAL	GRAND	LOAFING	
NOTHING EXTRA		SIGHTSEEING	
BEST ON THE MAP		BORROWING MONEY	
THE WEATHER IS		I NEED	
WARM	COOL	MONEY	YOU
WET	DRY	SLEEP	REST
PLEASANT		A GOOD JOB	
DREARY		$1,000,000	
THE FOLKS ARE		WILL SEE YOU	
NICE	SILLY	SOON	
QUIET	NOISY	LATER	
ENTERTAINING		NEXT WEEK	
FULL OF PEP		ON	
I'M FEELING		GIVE MY REGARDS TO	
FINE	WELL	MA AND DAD	
BUM	SICK	THE CHILDREN	
BLUE	HAPPY	MY CHUMS	
VERY LONESOME		EVERYBODY	

CHECK ITEMS DESIRED

BEACHES

Paul Éluard, like his fellow surrealists, was an avid deltiologist, a collector of postcards. He traded and shared cards with colleagues; disassembled old postcard albums in order to add to his own collection; rescued the erotic cards he found pasted on the walls of an old house; and took weekend excursions with André Breton to comb flea markets for illustrated ephemera. Once, he supposedly traded a Dalí painting with Georges Sadoul for two hundred postcards.

In his essay "Les plus belles cartes postales" (1933), Éluard celebrates the postcard as a window into the collective unconscious and as fecund soil from which new artworks might germinate. "Postcards," he writes, "do not constitute a popular art. At most, they are the small change left over from art and poetry. But this small change sometimes suggests the idea of gold."

But Éluard's collection speaks less to the desires and fantasies of the masses than to his own. His cartophilia was in part a response to the end of his marriage with Gala, who left him for Dalí. Pining for her, Éluard turned to the fantasy women on postcards, who, in a sense, replaced Gala as his muse. The cards in the category of "Love" reflected his own psychological reality. Éluard writes, "Under two burning hearts, the inscription: *United for Life*, the sender had crossed out *for Life*, thus depriving the Other of the idea of death, of that last drop of living blood." Love, too, was an object of exchange. Perhaps for this reason, Éluard continued to exchange erotic postcards with Gala long after she had left him.

ANIMALS

I collect haphazardly, sometimes because I am drawn to the colours on certain cards: the burgundy and bright yellow sails of ships docked at Le Havre; the grey of a group of donkeys; and the azure sky behind the old Notre Dame de Paris. I also use postcards as notepads: on the verso side of cards showcasing book cover designs, I scribble fragments of essays, stories, and novels.

After a year of collecting, I began to see postcards everywhere—in artworks, in literary texts, in films. Now I even see postcards in my sleep. During the day I read about John Stezaker's surrealist series of "inserts"—in which a vintage postcard is superimposed on a film still or black-and-white photograph, so that a cascading waterfall appears in the middle of a trial scene and crashing waves interrupt an exchange between two individuals—and at night I dream that my own face and the faces I see around me have been partially masked by a carefully aligned postcard.

RECTO — LAKE IN THE CLOUDS, ROCKIES

To Hilda Rank, Tooting Common, London

August 9, 1907

Dear Hilda,

You cannot imagine what a wonderful sight it is to have these enormous masses of rock all around you. I have not yet seen the tops of the very high mountains for they are all in the clouds. Will write tomorrow. Dick.

FLOWERS

When postcards first became coveted collectors' items in the late nineteenth century, they democratized the culture of collecting, due to their cheapness and ubiquity. Postcards of cityscapes and metropolitan scenes made it possible for anyone to create a personal atlas of the city and thereby chart the urban transformations taking place around them. Like these nineteenth-century deltiologists, I sometimes wandered down streets and compared the view on a postcard with the scene before me, so that even as the image highlighted what had disappeared, it simultaneously offered a kind of pictorial continuity. Other times, I superimposed a postcard on a completely different site, so that the picture replaced the view before me. In this way, the Southbank Centre, a place that once evoked tremendous sadness, eventually reminded me of a desert garden.

STREETSCAPES

The American photographer Walker Evans amassed over nine thousand postcards in his lifetime and engaged with them in his own work. Not only did Evans use postcards to determine the themes of his projects, but he also produced his own photographic postcards of simple, anonymous buildings, and published photo essays—illustrated with cards from his collection—that recorded the history of deltiology and provided a pictorial tour of American cities. Evans also recreated the scenes depicted on certain postcards from the same vantage point, thus foregrounding the changes wrought by time. Writing for *Fortune* in 1962, Evans described the picture postcard as a "folk document."

Beginning in the late 1950s, Evans presented postcard slide shows, first for friends in his New York City apartment. The postcard images would be blown up to the size of an entire wall and projected in the dark, as if in a cinema. Later, when invited to lecture at Yale and the Metropolitan Museum of Art about his career in photography, he gave postcard presentations instead. Evans invited his audiences to walk into the pictures, to see their own shadows layered on the streetscape of the past. As he explained, "one can, in effect, re-enter these printed images, and situate oneself upon the pavements in downtown Cleveland, Omaha or Chicopee Falls, Massachusetts."

PAINTINGS

Prior to 1902, the back side of the postcard was reserved for the address, and the message had to be squeezed into the margins next to the picture. In 1902, the British Post Office launched the "divided back" postcard, allowing the message to be written on one half of the verso, alongside the address, thus reserving the recto side for the photograph or illustration. This change, combined with new printing techniques, led to the dominance of the image.

RECTO — CRUE DE LA SEINE, JANVIER 1910

To Mademoiselle Fernande Henrienne, Place Cambronne, Paris
March 29, 1912
Il est inutile que vous vous dérangez pour moi, car il m'est com-
plètement impossible de rien pouvoir me préparer pour cette
semaine. Mes amitiés à vous.

WATERFALLS

In *You See I Am Here After All* (2008), the American artist Zoe
Leonard used approximately four thousand vintage postcards of
Niagara Falls to create a panoramic grid that ripples across the
gallery walls. The mass-produced touristic views are nearly iden-
tical, though there are variations in colours and perspective. In
Survey (2012), more than six thousand postcards of Niagara Falls
are stacked in towering piles. "We use things," Leonard writes,
"to communicate complex ideas, feelings; it is a dense, compact,
potent language, the language of the found object."

Hand-coloured, cropped, and manipulated—sometimes with
rainbows painted in to augment the beauty of the scene—these
postcards exemplify how the idealized imagery of a singular site is
constructed, polished, and disseminated via the tourist shop. Over
time, the Niagara Falls have been reshaped by erosion and human
intervention. But the postcards do not record such changes. The pictures, for all their minute differences, portray an unvarying cultural
construction. It is as if the natural wonder of the falls has remained
a frozen thing of beauty, perpetually covetable and collectible.

In much the same way, postcards of cities in the late nineteenth
and early twentieth centuries romanticized and reframed the urban
scene, clearing it of unsightly signs of poverty and modernization.

Paris thus became the prosperous centre of leisure and glamour, and Old Amsterdam with its concentric canals came to represent the city, even as the canals of other districts were filled in and canal-side houses torn down to make way for new developments.

RECTO— CLAPHAM COMMON, LONDON

To Miss Alice Taylor, Watford
July 10, 1905
Dear Alice,
Thanks for P.C. sometime ago. You have not told me what local ones you have got, so I do not know if you have this one or not. Best love, Nance.

OBJECTS

She stands on a hill with the others and watches as their city burns. The plumes of smoke have blackened the sky, and orange flames consume the frail forms of the buildings. All around them are scattered the possessions that they were able to rescue in the aftermath of the earthquake.

Her eyesight is blurred by resentment and shock as she looks at the lounging woman, who relaxes on the grass as though she were watching a film. Her own mind is bombarded by the images of all that she could not save, all the lives buried under the rubble of homes that will be rebuilt into utterly unrecognizable spaces.

ISLANDS

At the start of Antonio Tabucchi's short story "So Long," the narrator, Taddeo, sorts through his collection of postcards, searching for ones he might be able to send to friends on an upcoming trip. Taddeo playfully mismatches the images with the messages, thereby creating strange juxtapositions. On a postcard showing Robinson Island, he writes, "We're on Timultopec"; on one depicting towers, "This is the Machu Picchu mountain range."

All the cards are signed "Taddeo and Isabel," Isabel being the narrator's partner, with whom he was supposed to have travelled to South America. But she is no longer here. Taddeo packs her photograph in the suitcase with the postcards, so it'll be as if she were accompanying him on the trip.

Tabucchi's works are frequently marked by the experience of loss, of the dissonance between what is and what might have been. The *cartolina* here registers distance: between here and there, origin and destination; between one person's present and another person's past; between fantasy and reality. When the postcard is held in the hands, that distance might be temporarily bridged. But in the end, the object reaffirms the pastness of what has already gone.

At the train station, en route to the airport, Taddeo meets a young ice cream seller—also named Taddeo—and gives all his postcards to this boy who dreams of travelling the world when he grows up. The boy, stunned with the unexpected gift, thanks the older man. One day, he might forward the postcards to his own friends; or he might present them to a stranger who, like Taddeo, has suffered losses for which the collection offers fleeting consolation.

RECTO—ST PAUL'S CATHEDRAL

To Miss Harradine, E. Worthing

August 9, 1905

Sorry she has not been so well. I'm afraid it will be very awkward for me to be without E. the first week I am home. I shall not be equal to doing anything without a little help just at first, if I am to avoid relapses, for the journey will be rather an undertaking. Much love, H. B.

RIVERS

Picture postcards abound in the oeuvre of British artist Tacita Dean. Many of her projects involve revising or reframing the postcard, so that the once-static image begins to move in entirely new ways.

In *The Russian Ending* (2001), comprised of twenty photographic postcards portraying natural and anthropogenic disasters, Dean annotated the black-and-white images with film directions—"string music," "pan down"—thus infusing them with new narrative potential. It is strange to imagine people sending pictorial representations of death and destruction to loved ones. Perhaps the ubiquity of such images dampens their effect and expunges from collective memory the horrors of battlefields, explosions, and shipwrecks. Or perhaps they are a reminder that loss is always imminent.

Dean's *c/o Jolyon* series (2012–13)—my favourite of her postcard projects—is likewise preoccupied with catastrophe. It features one hundred prewar postcards of the German town of Kassel, which was blitzed by Allied bombing raids during WWII. Using photographs taken of the exact same locations, Dean overpainted the pictures with gouache and added details of the modern, postwar city—apartment buildings, cars, streetlamps. The result was a layered montage of the real past and the imagined present.

Dean's elegiac photographs and films are often preoccupied with such processes of disappearance or disintegration. A central irony of her work, as I see it, lies in the fact that these meditations on loss depend, in part, on the chance recovery of lost things. Dean trawls flea markets for vintage ephemera, and the serendipitous encounters lend new meaning to these objects that were once adrift amongst other urban detritus.

Like the surrealist *objet trouvé*, the postcard presents a series of absences—the nameless photographer, the unknown writer and recipient; it is constituted by what is unknown. But this opacity is irrelevant, because the found image is really about the person viewing it. As Dean remarks, "art works best when it responds to the autobiography of the viewer." Much like a dog following a trail in a zigzagging manner—to use Sebald's analogy—we follow the memory or thought triggered by the randomly discovered image. The creative act commences when we allow ourselves to be interrupted by the accidental, to be guided by pure contingency.

RUINS

I am attempting to think through the postcard, with dozens of images strewn across the desk before me. Yet I struggle to complete the essay. Where can I find the space for the contributions of Walter Benjamin, Aby Warburg, Jacques Derrida, W. G. Sebald, Agnès Varda, Susan Hiller, and David Opdyke? The collection remains incomplete, continually shifting as items are added or removed, and categories redefined. What strikes me about postcards is precisely this: their multiplicity and irreducibility, their tendency to expand outward, beyond the rectangular frame, into something infinitely arresting.

RECTO—RUINS CHURCH AND CASTLE ABERDOUR

To Mrs Duncan, Stockbridge
[date obscured]
Dear Bell,
I will be down on Sunday afternoon. Will you be going out. Pull the blind down so that I will know before I go. Night dear, Jean.

LIGHTHOUSES

The Japanese-born conceptual artist On Kawara dedicated his career to marking time. His projects took on ritualistic or diaristic qualities—art making as the quotidian practice of recording time. For his renowned *Today* series, Kawara created monochromatic canvases using traditional Japanese lacquering techniques, with fourteen to eighteen layers of acrylic paint. On these backgrounds, he used white paint to inscribe the date on which the work was made. If Kawara had not completed a painting by midnight, he would destroy it, as it would no longer be a painting of "today." Occasionally, he made two paintings in a day; rarely, three paintings. For another project, he sent telegrams with nothing except the message, "I am still alive."

In the *I Got Up* series, produced between 1968 and 1979, Kawara mailed thousands of postcards to acquaintances, with the rubber-stamped time of the exact hour and minute he woke up that day. He travelled extensively, and the messages chart his peripatetic wanderings. "I GOT UP AT 6.12 A.M.," he writes from Hong Kong; "I GOT UP AT 12.11 P.M.," from Quito, Ecuador.

The postcards form a self-portrait, an archive of the body's rhythms, its movements and moments of repose. They are also a way of structuring time, possibly of transcending it. As Tom McCarthy writes of the *Today* series, what the work "iterates is its own time, minus the time. What has actually been kidnapped, held to ransom, by the work is time." Is this not the function of writing, too? The essay a repository of stray thoughts; the fictional scene a tableau of fleeting emotions; the poem a frieze of remembered acts. We write—on postcards, in notebooks, on screens—to capture time.

When I finish flipping through the exhibition catalogue of Kawara's works, it is already late afternoon. There is golden sunlight and early spring warmth. I tuck a few blank postcards into a book and follow Kawara out the door. I mentally chart a route along the water. Perhaps somewhere along the way, there will be a café with an empty table, where I might write a postcard with this message: "I got up. I went. I read. I am alive."

Leanne Betasamosake Simpson

THE BREATHING LANDS

After the eagle and on my way home, I stopped at the house on the lake where you were staying. Tú y mi. Sitting in the bush, spreading out the pieces between us, the ones that broke us, the twenty years since the last time we were together. Your dead mama. The ones that didn't show up. The sacrifices. Yours always bigger than mine. You always bigger than me. You crying effortlessly and pulling it all out—the betrayal, the letdown, the pain. Me not feeling at all and staying inside myself. You trusting me with the mess of your life; me trusting you with very little.

You are speaking from the ossuary. There is blood on your hands, and death sits beside you. The atrocities are piling up. You chose to fight with your life, and I see the bullet holes. The mosquito bites. The bruises.

You. Valuing the intensity of anger, resentment, and sadness as fuel for movement. You made your choices. You wouldn't have it any other way, you say over and over.

Me. Trained by self-care memes, $175-an-hour unilateral friends whose only job is to centre me. I know boundaries and attachment styles and emotional maturity. I know the difference between intimacy and intensity. I see the cracks and the looping pedal, the wounds and the scars, as the programmed drum machine drives the melody forward. I see the repetition that leads to the wreckage. I see you, surprised by the mess you have draped yourself in, surprised at how things have turned out, after you set them up to turn out no other way.

I can see you, and you are unaware of me.

And still there is a nakedness to all of this, in the bush, beside the lake, us spreading out the pieces. What you are asking of me, you cannot give in return.

In that moment, with your tears and the mosquitoes, holding your hand, I knew I'd love you forever, and I was able to not get caught up in your spectacle. That was your gift to me. It was clear that I also speak from the ossuary, but my ossuary looks different from yours. So different it's been obfuscated for most of my life, but not anymore.

We both left Terra Santa.

You went south, back to your revolution.

And I made a promise to myself to go to the Breathing Lands.

Mitchell Consky

NOTES FROM GRIEF CAMP

In June of 2022, four boys bonded inside a summer-camp cabin.

After throwing loose shirts into cubbies and spreading sleeping bags onto sandy mattresses, a game of tag around the bunk beds quickly evolved into "the floor is lava."

Concealed within the laughter, however, was a link these four boys, all between the ages of five and seven, didn't yet know about: each of them had lost a father. And I, their camp counsellor for the weekend, had lost mine too.

But "lost" wasn't the right word.

As my co-counsellors and I learned from our training a few weeks earlier, being specific with language was imperative at grief camp. It was better to avoid any euphemisms like "passed away" and "lost," as they could inadvertently add confusion to the despair. In a child's mind, when something is lost, it can also be found. Our fathers would not be found.

"Do you know why you're all here?" asked a social worker, our group's clinical lead, once the boys had settled into silence. Afternoon sunlight rippled over the wooden floor we sat on.

"To have the best time ever!" the youngest replied. "And to play basketball!"

"Yes, that's true," the social worker said. "But there's another reason you're all here … Every single kid at this camp, including some of your counsellors, has had someone really important to them die."

The boys looked at one another, unsure of what to say next.

The ensuing days at this summer camp in McKellar, Ontario, a two-and-a-half-hour ride north of Toronto, would be full of traditional camper activities. More than a hundred boys and girls would climb the high ropes, jump into the lake for polar bear dips, and roast s'mores around campfires. But beneath the cheery surface of the conventional childhood experience, this was a different type of program. Here, a group of grieving kids—and the adults overseeing them—would try to find solace in the outdoors.

*

I first heard about Camp Erin a little more than a year after my father's funeral. A friend whose dad had also died sent me a link to the program, telling me the organization was recruiting volunteers. It is the largest national bereavement program for youth grieving the death of a parent or sibling.

The program was created by the Eluna Network, an organization that provides resources for children affected by death, and is offered in every city that has a Major League Baseball team. This bit of trivia isn't a coincidence: one of its founders, Jamie Moyer, is a former MLB pitcher.

The annual weekend was inspired by Erin Metcalf, a fifteen-year-old girl Moyer and his wife, Karen, first met in the late '90s through the Make-a-Wish Foundation. Erin had lung cancer. When she was hospitalized, she repeatedly expressed her concern for other visiting children as well as her own siblings, saying that she wanted to ensure they received the necessary support as they, too, navigated this scary reality. When Erin died at the age of seventeen in 2002, the Moyers felt that creating a "grief camp" to fulfill Erin's wishes would be a fitting tribute. And since then, hundreds of summer camps throughout North America have offered their facilities every year for the free weekend program.

As great as that all sounded, I felt hesitant about volunteering. I didn't doubt the program's merits; I grew up attending camp in northern Ontario, and it offered some of the most important experiences of my young life. But I couldn't reconcile the mix of bereavement and summer camp. What would we do—sit around a campfire and cry into each other's shoulders? As counsellors, would we spew platitudes about grief dissolving with time? Would there be moments of emotional vulnerability that I wouldn't know how to respond to? Most of all, I wondered if I'd really be able to help any of those kids experiencing the death of a loved one so early in life.

My father died when I was twenty-five. I was young by most standards but old enough to see that I was privileged to grow up with him. The kids at the camp were dealing with something different. They were going through not only the loss of a loved one but the absence of opportunity. They were grieving not only what they'd had but what they would never be able to experience: a father or mother teaching them how to drive, or cheering at their high school graduation, or celebrating their first job.

Moreover, I knew there would also be children at the camp grieving the loss of a sibling, something I couldn't relate to. What I would soon recognize, however, was that grief is not an exclusive club, and that everyone, no matter their experience, is invited to its miseries—as well as its joys.

*

Adults don't tend to deal well with death. Yes, it's in our shows, our songs, our art, our novels. But real deaths, the ones that take those we love, can feel taboo. We avoid talking about how loss feels, as though keeping the words out of our mouths will also keep the thoughts out of our minds. A 2019 survey conducted by online medical resource WebMD found that those experiencing grief often feel rushed to "get over it." Nearly three-quarters of all respondents had grieved a death within the past three years, and a little more than half said they felt expected to "move on" soon after, often as early as three months following the loss.

Adults have spent years immersed in our culture's troubled relationship with death. We may not like the various boundaries this relationship imposes, but we have been conditioned to accept them. For children, it's different. Nicky Seligman, a child-and-adolescent grief counsellor and the clinical director of Camp Erin Toronto for the summer of 2022, said it comes down to how bereavement is conceptualized. "I think there's so many misconceptions and myths in society and in the media," she told me over the phone. Our depictions tend to be rigid and simplistic: when referring to the way grief is often portrayed on screen, with characters in all-black clothing, or a grieving lover falling to their knees before a rain-soaked grave, Seligman used the term "one dimensional." That version of grief is something that a character trudges through until they arrive at the other side, a challenge to overcome.

"When you're working with kids, a lot of it is about debunking some of those myths and helping them really understand that dynamic experience of grief and all of the different feelings and behaviours and experiences they may have," Seligman said.

Grief is non-linear. One day, three years after a death, grief can return and feel as extreme as it did in the immediate aftermath of the loss. The ultimate difference between child grief and adult grief, she said, is how children will re-grieve throughout their lives.

For a young child experiencing the death of a parent, "their cognitive abilities are going to grow and change," Seligman said. At first, the finality of death might not register as clearly, but their understanding of that finality will mature with age; the implications of a loved one's physical absence will become more pronounced as they grow older.

"Part of that process is meeting kids where they're at," she said. "And helping them explore those questions and meet their developmental needs."

I faced something similar in my first moments at Camp Erin, when we sat in that circle in the cabin after the kids were told, for the first time, that most of the camp was grieving the death of someone special.

"You too?" the youngest asked, his big eyes peering my way.

"Yeah. Me too."

"Who?"

"My dad."

His little face formed an expression of empathy that seemed beyond his years. "How did he die?"

"Cancer," I said.

"What's cancer?" asked another camper.

"It's a disease where your body shuts down from bad cells that spread," I said. "It was really hard and scary."

Another part of our training—which took the form of online and in-person classes—was to lean into open dialogue like this and express vulnerabilities too often bottled up. This, we were told, would make children feel less alone in their own confusion.

Andrea Warnick is a registered psychotherapist, nurse, and thanatologist (or death researcher) who facilitated Camp Erin Toronto's training. She explained that transparency and inclusion are proven to lessen a child's sense of isolation while grieving. "It's not a child's job to open these conversations," she said. "That's an adult responsibility—to start the dialogue, to teach kids that we can talk about these really hard things."

When adults avoid engaging in these conversations with children, "we're making something that is already a really difficult and heartbreaking experience that much harder," she said. "We're losing the opportunity to clarify for them that, yeah, this really sucks, this is really hard for the adults too.

"It doesn't look like the adults are having a hard time, but it is hard. And it's natural that you're feeling what you're feeling. There's nothing you could have done to stop this."

*

"The north wind blows if you love chocolate ice cream!" shouted Ken, the program director, a bearded, high-energy guy campers naturally gravitated toward. He was standing with a megaphone at the centre of a field, surrounded by more than a hundred kids and volunteers.

The moment he called out, all the chocolate ice cream lovers launched off, running across the field to find another spot in the circle.

"The north wind blows" is a simple icebreaker. Personally, I prefer vanilla, but my campers grabbed my arms and yanked me for the sprint. One camper jumped on for a piggyback as we cannoned across the field.

"The north wind blows if…you can't wait to do the polar bear dip tomorrow morning!" Ken yelled.

I would find out later that none of my four campers actually knew what a polar bear dip was. Even so, they once again pulled me along. Spring sunshine beamed down on us, and the branches of surrounding trees swayed in the light breeze.

At first, Ken carried on with gentle prompts along these lines. But, slowly, things began turning serious.

"The north wind blows if…" He paused for a second or two longer, and his voice softened. "You miss someone you love."

Every camper, this time, and many staff changed spots in the circle. Ken started getting more specific.

"The north wind blows if…your mother died."

Kids looked around. A silence settled. At a slower pace this time, a group of boys and girls, scattered throughout the field, shuffled to new spots. As did a cluster of adults.

The campers exchanged glances, noticing all the other kids who had shared a similar experience. Before this weekend, many of them had probably never met another person their own age whose mom had died.

"The north wind blows if…your father died."

I crouched down next to my boys, who were staying close, as if afraid of the sudden change of tone. "That's all of us," I said gently.

Two of them grabbed my hands, one of them grabbed an arm, and another hung on for the piggyback.

Together, we moved to another spot in the circle.

*

When talking about how kids experience grief, Warnick described it as a puddle: something easy to jump in and out of. For adults, grief can feel more like an ocean, its vastness debilitating.

Children, Warnick explained, can abruptly transition from feeling devastated one moment to joyful the next. This is a healthy and normal approach to the messiness of grief, which doesn't abide by a "neat and tidy" narrative. Happiness doesn't disqualify grief, she said. "Happiness is part of grief."

Adults, meanwhile, are less able to transition from one emotion to the next. "I think a common myth in grieving adults—and I see this in [older] teens a fair bit too—is this 'black hole phenomenon,'" Warnick said. This is where grievers believe that if they feel the full intensity of their bereavement, they are going to get swallowed whole and remain stuck. The irony is that this fear of getting stuck becomes the real trap.

In denying despair, "there's an entire blunting out of feeling that happens," she said. People may not feel the grief, for instance, but they also won't feel the joy or the gratitude. Warnick said the only way to experience one end of the emotional spectrum—the positive feelings that grief does not disqualify—is by "opening it all up."

I could relate. After my father died, I remember armouring my mind against the pain. The result was a head-to-toe numbness that prevented me from feeling anything at all. The numbness dissolved only days after my dad's funeral, when I let out an unrestrained cry.

It happened on a hike, surrounded by trees. Somehow, the spring leaves and open air seemed to offer permission to unblock the emotions I had lost access to. I sat down and leaned against an old cedar. The sensation was physical at first—a loosening of my shoulders, an expansion in my tight chest. This bodily unravelling cleared the way for the mental turmoil I had pushed aside. It leaked out; then it cascaded. I wept and yelled. When it was over, I smiled. A lightness carried me through the following days.

Surrender such as this, Warnick said, is key. It's the ultimate difference between how adults and children process death. "Many kids, especially the younger they are, [are] just going to allow themselves to [experience it.] And it's going to happen," she said.

This can look a million different ways: withdrawal, exhaustion, anger, fixation, depression, and distraction are all behaviours that grief counsellors like Warnick identify in kids. But these periods of negative reaction are often less prolonged than they would be for grown-ups.

Warnick believes this comes from an inherent understanding that kids grasp quicker: that emotional pain is "not going to stay." Recognizing this allows grievers to feel their pain and move through it. "I think that that's a huge [lesson] for adults from kids—that, actually, there's real utility in allowing yourself sometimes to even be brought to your knees."

*

After lunch one day at Camp Erin, sitting in the cabin, the social worker prompted us to reveal photos of our fathers, which most of the boymothers had packed.

What followed was a sort of show-and-tell session, featuring fathers who had died of various causes, from tragic accidents to illness. I showed a picture of my dad, smiling as he sat on a swing set, wearing a blue button-up, his legs pointed toward the sky.

Eventually, my co-counsellor, Julia, showed a photo of a young man in a yellow shirt. He looked about my age. "This is my son, Clayton," she told us.

Julia was a mother of three boys—two of whom I actually knew, because, coincidentally, we went to the same summer camp growing up. Her oldest, Clayton, died of an accidental drug over-dose in September 2017. He was nine days away from his twenty-third birthday.

"This was an extremely devastating and traumatic and unbelievably sad thing for me, my husband, and my two other sons," she told me later.

Julia first volunteered at Camp Erin Toronto in June 2019, after learning about the program through her involvement in a group for moms who had had a child die. Her first experience at Camp Erin, she told me, was therapeutic and allowed her to experience her bereavement fully. She was caught off guard by how the kids around her could switch from despair to joy, effortlessly moving from making emotional confessions to giggling in canoes. Julia said helping those children opened her eyes to how she could reclaim parts of her own life. "You're so in your head about your own grief, and then you see these kids and you want to (a) help them and (b) you see how they just turn on and off," she said.

Julia had been on leave from her job for nearly two years before she went to Camp Erin. After that first weekend, she felt ready to go back to work. In June 2022, after a pandemic-enforced hiatus, she returned to camp as a counsellor for a second time.

Julia and I became fast friends. We were a team, stopping our four troublemakers from their inclinations to jump off high structures, tip canoes, and, once, eat bowls of white sugar for breakfast. Her instincts for ensuring the kids always had enough sunscreen, hydration, and nutrition at the dinner table (the last one being no easy thing to guarantee at buffet-style meals), along with her boundless patience, intimately reminded me what she was: a veteran mother of three boys.

Julia noted the quick bond the little guys felt toward me. "They heavily related to you," she reflected during our phone call. She told me that, over that weekend away, I was able to fill in as a male figure for our group, a facilitator of mischief and horseplay. "The fact that you were there and you had lost a father too—that was something that helped them connect really quickly."

As healing as the experience was, however, Julia also noted a disconnect between the kids and her experience with grief. "I remember telling them that my son died, and I think it was something they almost couldn't understand," she said.

What they did understand, however, was that they had permission to feel however they chose to and to lean into the excitement and fun. Our boys rolled down grassy hills. They drummed the table in the mess hall. They found and named three caterpillars (Gerry, Larry, and Harry). They danced on stage for the camp talent show. They raced from one activity to the next. It was all exhausting. But it was also energizing.

Julia recalled a specific moment, after we paddled canoes, when the youngest boy turned to her and said, to her astonishment, "This is the best day of my life."

Recalling this comment, Julia emphasized the absurdity. "He's at a grieving camp!"

*

The lake shimmered with an orange glow as the whole camp sat before a fire pit and an evening wind rolled in, carrying the forest's aroma of cedar and oak. In place of a fire, however, we all had our attention on a large blue board. Painted on a white piece of fabric strung to the top were the words "In Memory Of…"

As Ken softly strummed an acoustic guitar, cabin groups were called for what was known as the "photo ceremony." One at a time, children of all ages revealed a photo of the person they were grieving. They declared, sometimes in quaking voices, how the person had died, before clipping the image to the board.

"This is my dad. He died of suicide."

"This is my brother. He died of a drug overdose."

"This is my mother. She died of cancer."

Soon enough, every inch of the board was plastered with smiling faces.

At this moment, none of my own grief was pointing inward. There was a feeling of expansiveness that emanated as my campers sat close to me, all of us watching the scene unfold.

Julia, sitting to my left, threw an arm around my shoulder, and the simple—maybe even clichéd—lesson of the weekend suddenly became pronounced: togetherness makes sorrow a little easier to bear.

When our cabin was called, our four boys stood up and spoke bravely about their fathers. After them, I shared the image of my dad on the swing. Then I bent down and clipped it to the board.

Seeing him there, amid all the mothers and fathers, brothers and sisters, sons and daughters, I reminded myself he wasn't lost. And neither were we.

Katherine Ashenburg

HOW WE SAID GOODBYE

So, you've lost the person you loved, but you've also
lost the way to send them on. You lost the farewell.
—Angela Sumegi

When twenty-one-year-old Revere Osler died at the Battle of Passchendaele in 1917, all his parents could do was bring flowers to his bedroom. His father, the great Canadian clinician Sir William Osler, wanted to go at once to Europe, but there was no point. His only child had been buried immediately. In England, where Osler was a professor of medicine at Oxford, morale was so low in 1917 that memorial services for soldiers were considered unpatriotic. Also bad for morale was the wearing of black, as was the strict, protective schedule of seclusion for the mourner.

To make a distinction that has fallen out of use, the Oslers grieved profoundly, but they could not mourn. Dictionaries define "grieving" as the private feelings of sorrow that a death arouses. "Mourning" describes the outward expression of those feelings in practices and rituals, often done communally.

Like the Oslers, the bereaved in the early days of COVID-19 were forbidden to mourn. We could sorrow privately, of course, but funerals and graveside services were either banned or drastically limited. The Jewish shiva, the Irish wake, and the Muslim custom of prayers around the corpse in a mosque all became impossible or, at best, significantly deformed. So were the ritual washing of the dead prescribed in many cultures, the Hindu funeral pyres along the Ganges, and countless other mourning customs.

*

Anne Kingston died unexpectedly on February 12, 2020. A prize-winning writer at *Maclean's* and the author of two books, she was sixty-two. Anne's friends and colleagues were shocked: her death had followed her cancer diagnosis with such swiftness that most of us did not even know she was ill. We were told that a memorial was planned for March. None of us doubted that one would be possible.

Soon after Anne's death, I spent a few weeks in Mexico. Outbreaks of a mysterious coronavirus dominated the news more and more, but, at least on the surface, life went on as before in the colonial towns I visited. After the initial surprise and sadness, I found it hard to believe that Anne was really gone. We had not been in each other's closest circles, but whenever we managed to meet for dinner, we fell immediately into an easy intimacy where everything was on the table: love, work, friendship, family, the problems of the world.

In those first weeks, I couldn't understand that we would never again meet at a restaurant, where Anne would comment with discerning relish on the food before returning to the discussion at hand—which we never finished because it inevitably branched off into something equally fascinating. Nor could I comprehend that I had read the last of her penetrating, original views in *Maclean's*, on everything from Bill Cosby to women who regretted having children, from IKEA to Michael Ignatieff. Increasingly focused on gender issues, Anne approached topics in her own inimitable way. Covering the trial of Jian Ghomeshi, for example, she dared to analyze his lawyer Marie Henein's appearance (her toe cleavage and "almost architectural hair...reminiscent of the black crest of a red-whiskered bulbul" were declarations of power and control).

One soft evening in Puebla, I had an errand that involved crossing the main square, overlooked by the towering formality of the cathedral and lined with restaurants and shops. In the centre of the square, a band was playing for a troupe of dancers. To the traditional blend of violins, guitars of various sizes, trumpets, and a harp, the dancers stomped their heels on the wooden stage, dipped, bowed, pirouetted, and braided their way through their fellow performers. The men wore the short-jacketed costume of the *charro*, or horseman; the women, full white skirts with bands of yellow, their hair festooned with yellow flowers.

Watching them, I was suddenly overcome with tears for Anne, the first I had shed for her. I don't think we ever had a single conversation about Mexico; it was not one of our subjects. But something about the skill and the innocent joy of the performers evoked her. Shy in some ways, she was always ready to be delighted—by a wine, an outrageous pair of tights, a well-built sentence or argument. Although she was uncompromising and not afraid to be blunt, she was also, like the performers, generous. (When my first novel was published—but only after Anne had read it and approved—she insisted on taking me out to dinner to celebrate.) These are after-the-fact rationalizations for my tears. All I was conscious of in the square that night was the piercing thought that Anne would never be able to enjoy this lovely sight—or any other.

That was the start of my grieving. My mourning was another story. Needless to say, there was no memorial for Anne in March 2020.

*

Why did I feel something important had been left undone when we could not gather to lament and celebrate Anne? Surely my solitary grief was the more significant part of my bereavement—or so I thought. But it must mean something that almost every society has a communal ritual of farewell. The Hopi in Arizona bury their dead with no gathering or ceremony, but they are highly unusual in that respect. Often, the further a Protestant denomination is from Catholicism, the more minimal its funerals. Queen Victoria was disconcerted by the bare-bones Presbyterian leave-taking she witnessed for the father of her beloved gillie, John Brown. A small group stood in the hallway of the dead man's house, said a few prayers, and repaired with his coffin to the graveyard. The queen found it sadly inadequate, but at least Mr Brown was accompanied to his final destination.

There were no grief therapists or experts in mourning in the years that followed the First World War, so no one was counting the cost of the stifled rituals, the forbidden gatherings, the lack of acknowledgement given to the Oslers and other bereaved people. These days, research tells us that cultures with a rich menu of mourning customs and gatherings have significantly lower incidences of unresolved bereavement than societies where loss is a solitary affair. Standing in the presence of other mourners, even in a crowd of mostly strangers, is oddly crucial; a friend calls it "the terrible necessity of other people."

In at least the first year and a half of the pandemic, the death announcements in our newspapers often promised future memorials. I remember one in the *Globe and Mail* that said that a gathering would happen "when hugs are allowed." I don't know how many of those promises were fulfilled, but as the fear of congregating continued to ebb and flow through 2020, 2021, and 2022, I no longer expected that there would be a memorial for Anne. Her death had been overwhelmed by COVID, it seemed, and any feelings her family and friends had of being in limbo might well be permanent.

But in September 2022 I received an invitation from Tycho Manson, a friend of Anne's who had been in charge of her first, cancelled memorial. Two years and eight months after her death, a celebration of her life would take place at Hart House, on the campus of the University of Toronto. The organizers—Manson, Anne's brothers, David and Rob Kingston, and Peter Boyd, an ex-partner who remained a close friend—said they never doubted there would eventually be a gathering. The suddenness of her death had meant that almost no one was able to say goodbye, so all the more reason for a memorial. "We knew we had to have an event where we could mourn Anne as well as grieve her," Mason told me later over the phone.

Although he knows it's apocryphal, Boyd said that the legend of Mozart being dumped into the pauper communal grave spurred him on: he was determined that the pandemic would not squelch the celebration Anne deserved.

On October 12, I made my way to Hart House's Music Room, a wood-panelled rectangle lit by the late afternoon sun. The anthropologist Victor Turner once described ritual as the action that integrates a disturbed social group after a crisis. Were Anne's friends and family a disturbed social group, after all this time, and were we about to enact a ritual? To answer the second question first, our ancestors expected a ritual to be solemn, choreographed, and often sacred, so our gathering would not have made their cut. But for at least fifty years, secular mourners have gathered the dead person's community, provided food and drink, speeches and spontaneous anecdotes, often a slide show and music. It's our informal overhaul of Yeats's "custom and ceremony," and it seems to suit the times.

My sense of the people in the Music Room as a coherent group, and hardly a disturbed one, came into focus only gradually. At first, we stood, parked our wine glasses on high round tables while we accepted sliders and spring rolls, and did a certain amount of asking, "How did you know Anne?" There were colleagues from the *Financial Times* and *Maclean's*, as well as friends from unsuspected corners of her life. The speeches celebrated the little sister whose strong-mindedness and sense of justice surfaced early, the cool cousin who taught a younger one how to dress and find the best music, the aunt who instructed a niece in cooking and eating. There were wry memories of the writer who surrendered her article to an editor only at the very last minute and a shaggy-dog story from a long-ago boyfriend about a camping trip that went sideways. Over the heads of the speakers, at the front of the room, Anne presided in photographs: laughing, self-conscious, mischievous.

The combination of words and pictures brought her back to me, and I imagine to many others. After the speeches, we carried on in small clusters with more memories. By the time people began to leave, I felt I was part of a group that had suffered a bereavement and had given some comfort, most often unspoken, to one another.

In *The Greek Way of Death*, the classicist Robert Garland wrote that separation requires "vigorous and determined efforts on both sides: as the body must leave the group, so the group must leave the body." Anne's body had not been with us for a long time, but in what sense could we say farewell to Anne the person? The key is in Garland's words: "vigorous and determined efforts." First, we had to bring back the woman we enjoyed, admired, loved. We celebrated her, but that brought sorrow because we had a fresh sense of what we had lost. And that was as it should be. We brought Anne back to life so that, finally, we could mourn her departure.

CONTRIBUTORS' BIOGRAPHIES

KATHERINE ASHENBURG describes herself as a lapsed Dickensian, in that her work life began with a PhD thesis about Charles Dickens and Christmas. Since then, she has worked as a CBC Radio producer, the arts and books editor of the *Globe and Mail*, and, for the last few decades, as a freelance writer. She has written hundreds of articles in newspapers and magazines from *Toronto Life* to the *Times Literary Supplement*, on subjects that range from mourning to Nordic walking poles. Her award-winning non-fiction books include *Going to Town: Architectural Walking Tours in Southern Ontario*, *The Mourner's Dance: What We Do When People Die*, *The Dirt on Clean: An Unsanitized History*, and *All the Dirt: A History of Getting Clean* (for ages 9 to 12). She has also written three novels, published by Knopf Canada: *Sofie & Cecilia*, *Her Turn*, and *Margaret's New Look* (forthcoming, 2025).

JAMES CAIRNS is a staff writer at the *Hamilton Review of Books*, the community relations director for the Riverside Reading Series, and an associate professor in the Department of Indigenous Studies, Law and Social Justice at Wilfrid Laurier University. He is the author of three books on social and political theory, most recently, *The Myth of the Age of Entitlement: Millennials, Austerity, and Hope* (UTP, 2017). James's writing appears in various scholarly, literary, and political journals, including *Canadian Notes & Queries*, the *Montreal Review*, the *Marx & Philosophy Review of Books*, *Spring Magazine*, *Briarpatch*, TOPIA, and the *Journal of Canadian Studies*. James lives with his family in Paris, Ontario, where he is working on a collection of essays about crisis.

MITCHELL CONSKY is a Toronto-based writer and the author of *Home Safe: A Memoir of End-of-Life Care*. His work has appeared in *Reader's Digest Worldwide*, the *Globe and Mail*, the *Toronto Star*, *The Walrus*, BNN Bloomberg, and CTVNews.ca. When not working, his ideal escape is drifting on a canoe in Ontario's Algonquin Park. He lives in Toronto.

MICHELLE CYCA is a writer living in Vancouver on the unceded and ancestral homelands of the xʷməθkʷəy̓əm, Sḵwx̱wú7mesh Úxwumixw, and səlilwətaʔɬ peoples. She is currently a senior editor with *The Narwhal*, a contributing writer to *The Walrus*, and contributing editor to *Maclean's*. Her essays and journalism can also be found in the *Guardian*, *Chatelaine*, *IndigiNews*, and many other places. Her literary criticism can be found in *Quill & Quire*, the *Globe and Mail*, and the *Vancouver Sun*. Previously, she was the co-publisher and editor-in-chief of SAD Mag, a National Magazine Award–winning magazine celebrating Vancouver arts and culture. Michelle is a member of the Muskeg Lake Cree Nation in Treaty 6, Saskatchewan.

SADIQA DE MEIJER's poetry, essays, and short fiction have been published internationally. Her books include the poetry collections *Leaving Howe Island* and *The Outer Wards*, and *alfabet/alphabet: a memoir of a first language*, which was awarded a Governor General's Literary Award. Recurring themes in her writing include landscape, migration, motherhood, language, and spirituality. She is currently poet laureate of Katarohkwi/Kingston. "Found" is part of the essay collection *In the Field*, to be published by Palimpsest Press in 2025.

ARIEL GORDON (she/her) is a Winnipeg/Treaty 1 Territory–based writer, editor, and enthusiast. In 2019, *Treed: Walking in Canada's Urban Forests*, a collection of essays that combines science writing and the personal essay, was published by Hamilton's Wolsak & Wynn. It received an honourable mention for the 2020 Alanna Bondar Memorial Book Prize for Environmental Humanities and Creative Writing from ALECC. In 2022, Ariel's essays appeared in *Canadian Notes & Queries*, *Canthius*, and the *Winnipeg Free Press*. In spring 2024, her second book of creative nonfiction, *Fungal: Foraging in the Urban Forest*, was published by Wolsak & Wynn. The essay that appears in *Best Canadian Essays* was published in Calgary's *FreeFall* in spring 2023 and appears in *Fungal*.

LANA HALL is a journalist based in Toronto. Her essays and journalism appear in the *Globe and Mail*, *Maclean*'s, *Hazlitt*, *Maisonneuve*, *Canadian Business*, and various literary magazines.

Her work has been featured in the Top 5 of the Week and Editor's Pick series by *Longreads*. Much of her writing covers the urban affairs beat, but she has also written stories about the criminal justice system, climate change, labour, and provincial and municipal politics. She has received grants and recognition for her work from the Toronto Arts Council, the Ontario Arts Council, the Canada Council for the Arts, the Digital Publishing Awards, and the National Magazine Awards. Lana holds a bachelor's degree in journalism from Toronto Metropolitan University (formerly Ryerson) and an MFA in creative nonfiction from the University of King's College. Learn more about her work at www.lanahallwrites.com or follow her on X at @curiouslana.

HELEN HUMPHREYS is the author of four books of poetry, ten novels, and six works of creative nonfiction. She has won the Rogers Writers' Trust Fiction Prize, the City of Toronto Book Award, a Lambda Award for fiction, the CAA award for poetry, and most recently, the Matt Cohen Award from Writers' Trust in honour of her writing career. Her work has been translated and published in many countries, and has been optioned for opera, film, television, and the stage. Her latest book, *Followed By the Lark*, is a novel on Henry David Thoreau, published by HarperCollins Canada and Farrar, Straus and Giroux in February 2024. She lives and writes in Kingston, Ontario.

REBECCA KEMPE is a writer, zinester, and multidisciplinary artist from Ottawa, Ontario. Her work has been published in *flo.*, the *Ampersand Review*, *Sumac Literary Magazine*, and elsewhere. Her plays *Each on Our Side* and *Signal Breakdown* were performed in the 2019 and 2021 editions, respectively, of the Youth Infringement

Festival. She is the author of *There's Nothing to See Here/Nothing Happens Here*, a two-part zine which explores the stagnant (but at times welcome) stillness of the suburbs she grew up in, through photography and prose. More of her work can be found at www.rkempe.ca and you can find her online as @arbeeko.

JIIN KIM was born in Seoul, Korea, moved to Toronto, Ontario, at the age of nine, and has lived for the past sixteen years in St John's, Newfoundland. For many years, she took great joy in choosing and reading great children's literature to her sons. These marvellous stories inspired Jiin to write a book herself. *Lore Isle*, a middle-grade fantasy novel, was published by Nimbus in 2023. Jiin has written fiction and non-fiction short stories that have been published in anthologies, newspapers, and literary journals. She is currently working on an adult novel.

Jiin has a degree in fine art from the University of Toronto and continues to draw, paint, and create in mixed media. She has won Newfoundland and Labrador Arts and Letters awards in literary and visual arts divisions. Jiin has two jobs she loves— working at the library and teaching group fitness classes. Now that her children are grown, Jiin dotes on a pair of delightful rescue rabbits, constructing a rabbit-sized cardboard village in hopes of gaining their affection.

CHRISTINE LAI is a novelist and essayist who writes primarily on art and images. Her debut novel, *Landscapes*, is published by Doubleday Canada and by Two Dollar Radio in the United States. Her writings have appeared in *Joyland*, *The Ex-Puritan*, PRISM *international*, *Geist*, and *Necessary Fiction*. Christine holds a PhD in English literature from University College London.

JESSICA MOORE is an author and literary translator with a special interest in the shadowy corridors between languages and
between people. Her first book, *Everything, now* (Brick Books,
2012) is a love letter to the dead. *The Whole Singing Ocean* (Night-
wood, 2020) is a true story blending long poem, investigation,
sailor slang, and ecological grief. Her translations have been
nominated for the International Man Booker, the French-
American Foundation Translation Prize, and have won the UK's
Wellcome Prize and a PEN America Translation Award. Jessica
lives in Tkaronto/Toronto where she tends to her twins and her
urban garden. Her work-in-progress, *Porous*, is a memoir of
motherhood and art.

TOM RACHMAN is the author of five works of fiction: his bestselling debut, *The Imperfectionists* (2010), which was translated
into twenty-five languages; the critically acclaimed follow-up, *The
Rise & Fall of Great Powers* (2014); a story collection, *Basket of
Deplorables* (2017); a novel set in the art world, *The Italian Teacher*
(2018); and a novel-in-stories about writers, *The Imposters* (2023).

Born in London in 1974, then raised in Vancouver, Rachman
studied cinema at the University of Toronto and journalism at
Columbia University in New York. He worked at the Associated
Press as a foreign-news editor in its Manhattan headquarters,
then became a correspondent in Rome. He also reported from
India, Sri Lanka, Japan, South Korea, Egypt, Turkey and elsewhere.
To write fiction, he left the AP and moved to Paris, supporting
himself as an editor at the *International Herald Tribune*, the
global edition of the *New York Times*.

His writing has appeared in the *New York Times*, the *Atlantic*,
the *Washington Post*, the *Wall Street Journal*, and the *New Yorker*,

among other publications. Today, he is a contributing columnist at the *Globe and Mail*. He lives in London.

LEANNE BETASAMOSAKE SIMPSON is a Michi Saagiig Nishnaabeg writer, musician, intellectual, and member of Alderville First Nation. She is the author of eight previous books, including the novel *Noopiming: A Cure for White Ladies* and *Rehearsals for Living*, co-authored with Robyn Maynard.

VANCE WRIGHT is a reconnecting two-spirit member of the Tl'azt'en Nation and was raised on the unceded territories of the Sinixt Nation in what is colonially known as Nelson, BC. Currently residing in the occupied and unceded territories of the Musqueam, Squamish, and Tsleil-Waututh Nations in Vancouver, they are an artist, writer, and emerging curator who is pursuing their bachelor of fine arts at Emily Carr University of Art and Design.

PUBLICATIONS CONSULTED FOR THE 2025 EDITION

Aeon, The Ampersand Review, The Antigonish Review, Arc Poetry Magazine, BC Bookworld, Border Crossings, Brick, CAMEL, *Canadian Literature, Canadian Notes & Queries, Capilano Review, Corporate Knights, Dalhousie Review,* EVENT, *Exile Quarterly, The Ex-Puritan, The Fiddlehead, filling Station, FreeFall, Geist,* the *Globe and Mail, Grain, Granta, Hamilton Arts & Letters, Hazlitt, Herizons, Horseshoe, Leaf Magazine, Literary Review of Canada, Maisonneuve, The Malahat Review, The Nashwaak Review,* the *Newfoundland Quarterly, The New Quarterly, New York Times, Open Minds Quarterly, Parentheses, Peach Magazine, Periodicities, Prairie Fire,* PRISM *international, Queen's Quarterly, Quillette, Ricepaper Magazine, Riddle Fence, Room, Spacing, subTerrain, The /tɛmz/ Review, Toronto Life, The Tyee, Typescript, University of Toronto Quarterly, untethered magazine, The Walrus, The Windsor Review, yolk.*

ACKNOWLEDGEMENTS

"How We Said Goodbye" by Katherine Ashenburg first appeared in the *Literary Review of Canada*. Reprinted by permission of the author.

"My Struggle and 'My Struggle'" by James Cairns first appeared in *Canadian Notes & Queries*. Reprinted by permission of the author.

"Notes from Grief Camp" by Mitchell Consky first appeared in *The Walrus*. Reprinted by permission of the author.

"Big Babies" by Michelle Cyca first appeared in *The Walrus*. Reprinted by permission of the author.

"Found" by Sadiqa de Meijer first appeared in *The New Quarterly*. Reprinted by permission of the author.

"Rotten" by Ariel Gordon first appeared in *FreeFall*. Reprinted by permission of the author.

"We Are All Animals at Night" by Lana Hall first appeared in *Hazlitt*. Reprinted by permission of the author.

"The Boiler Room" by Helen Humphreys first appeared in *The New Quarterly*. Reprinted by permission of the author.

"The 'Beauty' of My Existence" by Rebecca Kempe first appeared in *The Ampersand Review*. Reprinted by permission of the author.

"Complimentary, Free of Charge" by Jiin Kim first appeared in *Room*. Reprinted by permission of the author.

"Now Must Say Goodbye" by Christine Lai first appeared in *Geist*. Reprinted by permission of the author.

"Shadow Face" by Jessica Moore first appeared in *Brick*. Reprinted by permission of the author.

"Confessions of a Literary Schlub" by Tom Rachman first appeared in the *Globe and Mail*. Reprinted by permission of the author.

"The Breathing Lands" by Leanne Betasamosake Simpson first appeared in *Brick*. Reprinted by permission of the author.

"Birth Stories, Adoption, and Myths" by Vance Wright first appeared in *The Ex-Puritan*. Reprinted by permission of the author.

EDITOR'S BIOGRAPHY

Emily Urquhart is the author of three books of nonfiction including the essay collection, *Ordinary Wonder Tales*, a finalist for the 2023 Hilary Weston Writers' Trust Prize for Nonfiction. She has a background in journalism and a doctorate in folklore and draws on both in her writing. She is a five-time National Magazine Award nominee for her journalistic work and has won gold and silver. She lives in Kitchener, Ontario, with her husband and two children, where she is a nonfiction editor for *The New Quarterly* and teaches creative writing and science communication at the University of Waterloo.